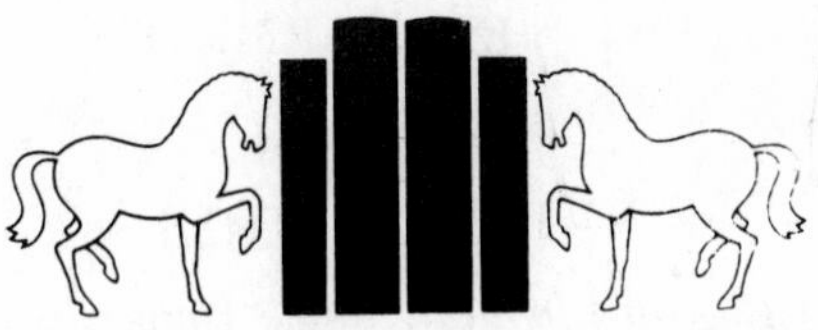

A BENN STUDY · DRAMA

THE NEW MERMAIDS

# The Rivals

THE NEW MERMAIDS

*General Editors*

BRIAN MORRIS

*Professor of English Literature in the University of Sheffield*

BRIAN GIBBONS

*Senior Lecturer in English in the University of York*

ROMA GILL

*Senior Lecturer in English Literature in the University of Sheffield*

# The Rivals

RICHARD BRINSLEY SHERIDAN

*Edited by*

ELIZABETH DUTHIE
*Lecturer in English, University College, Cardiff*

LONDON/ERNEST BENN LIMITED

NEW YORK/W. W. NORTON AND COMPANY INC.

*First published in this form 1979*
*by Ernest Benn Limited*
*25 New Street Square · Fleet Street · London · EC4A 3JA*
*& Sovereign Way · Tonbridge · Kent · TN9 1RW*



*Published in the United States of America by*
*W. W. Norton and Company Inc.*
*500 Fifth Avenue · New York · N.Y. 10036*

*Distributed in Canada by*
*The General Publishing Company Limited · Toronto*

*Printed in Great Britain*

**British Library Cataloguing in Publication Data**

Sheridan, Richard Brinsley
The rivals.—(New Mermaids).
1. Title 2. Duthie, Elizabeth
3. Series
822'.6 PR3682.R4

ISBN 0-510-34141-1
ISBN 0-393-90044-4 (U.S.A.)

# CONTENTS

## ACKNOWLEDGEMENTS

MY GREATEST DEBT, which is that of all students of Sheridan, is to the work of Cecil Price, in his editions of the dramatic works and of the letters. I have also made use of the editions of G. H. Nettleton (1906), R. L. Purdy (1935), and A. N. Jeffares (1967). The labours of G. W. Stone and C. B. Hogan, editors of Parts Four and Five of *The London Stage,* have made my task easier, and I have benefited from John Loftis's lively work on Sheridan.

I should like to thank the Syndics of the Cambridge University Library for permission to reproduce the title-page of their copy of the first edition of *The Rivals.* My thanks are also due to the staff of the following institutions: the Library, University College, Cardiff; the British Library; and the National Army Museum.

Brian Morris has advised on the text with his customary penetration and intelligence. I am grateful for the help of Michael Crump, and for the advice of my colleagues Roger Ellis and Peter Garside. It is to be counted among the least of his virtues that my husband, Michael Jubb, has been my most perceptive critic.

*Cardiff*
*March 1979*

E. D.

# INTRODUCTION

## THE AUTHOR

RICHARD BRINSLEY SHERIDAN was born in Dublin in 1751, the third son of Frances and Thomas Sheridan, who was then manager of the Theatre Royal there. In 1754, his parents left Dublin after the theatre was destroyed in a riot, and their debts mounted. Thomas had some success in England, and Scotland, as a teacher of elocution; Frances wrote a novel, *Sidney Bidulph* (1761), and a successful comedy, *The Discovery* (1763), in which Thomas acted. In 1764, however, the family went to France to escape their creditors, leaving the adolescent Sheridan an unhappy pupil at Harrow School, ashamed of his poverty and his shabby clothes.[1]

In 1770, Sheridan went to Bath with his father (his mother had died in France). There they met the Linley family, who taught singing and gave concerts. The eldest daughter, Elizabeth, unwilling to marry any of her several suitors, sought the young Sheridan's protection, and fled with him to France in 1772. On his return to England, Sheridan fought two duels with one of the suitors. The whole affair was elaborated in public gossip; and Sheridan's father, who thought the Linley family too low for his son to marry into, sent him away from Bath to study law. The couple kept up a correspondence, however, and in April 1773 they were married in London. Their parents were reconciled to the match, but since Sheridan thought it beneath his dignity as a gentleman to allow his wife to earn money by singing, the couple had little to live on. *The Rivals* was written in the hope of making at least six hundred pounds,[2] and first acted in January 1775. In the same year, Sheridan wrote *St Patrick's Day,* a short farce, and *The Duenna,* a comic opera, which was far more successful at the time than *The Rivals*. Already he was highly regarded as a playwright: when he was proposed for the Literary Club in 1777, Dr Johnson said that he had written 'the two best comedies of his age'.[3] When Garrick retired from the Drury Lane theatre in 1776, Sheridan became a shareholder and principal manager, borrowing heavily to do so. His success was crowned by *The School for Scandal* in 1777, and *The Critic* two years later.

His ambitions were political as well as literary. In 1780, he

[1] *Letters of Richard Brinsley Sheridan,* ed. Cecil Price (Oxford, 1966), I, no. 1.
[2] ibid., I, no. 33.
[3] Boswell, *Life of Johnson,* eds Hill and Powell (Oxford, 1934–50), III, 116.

became MP for Stafford, a 'venal borough' which he held until 1806.[4] For most of his parliamentary career, he was in opposition, and associated with the group of radical Whigs led by Charles James Fox. He attacked the savage penal code and the slave trade, and fought unsuccessfully for Catholic emancipation: his speeches against Warren Hastings, accused of extortion and cruelty in India, were triumphs of oratory. In the Regency Crisis of 1788, he was a principal adviser to the prince of Wales, who acted as a focus for the opposition to his father's government, and with whom Sheridan remained on good terms until near the end of his life.

He was part of a raffish, aristocratic set, heavy gamblers and hard drinkers. In 1789, he was described as 'a great gallant and intriguer among fine ladies' although 'a strange choice, having a red face, and as ill a look as I ever saw'.[5] He drifted apart from his wife, but when she died in 1792, he seems to have felt real grief.

Once an MP, he took less interest in the theatre; his last play, *Pizarro* (1799), an adaptation from the German, is feeble. In 1793–94, he had borrowed heavily to rebuild Drury Lane, and although his second wife, Esther Ogle, whom he married in 1795, brought him some money, he was unable to use it for his own purposes. His letters are studded with urgent appeals for money to Richard Peake, treasurer at the theatre: from Bognor, 1795, 'I have not a shilling at this Place and the Bills all unpaid': from the Star and Garter, Pall Mall, 1798, 'Send me pray two Pound or I shall be stuck here for my reckoning': 1802, 'Words cannot tell you the situation of this house there is not even a candle in it—or a little tea for Mrs S.! . . . if I am not assisted with £20 tonight Mrs S. will be distracted'.

'Borrow and fear not' (an isolated phrase in one of the letters to Peake)[6] can sum up Sheridan's attitude to money, and at the end of his life debts and troubles mounted on him. By 1806 he was frequently, perhaps chronically, drunk; he compromised his hitherto valued political independence by asking for a sinecure for his son, and himself accepted the Receiver-Generalship of the Duchy of Cornwall.[7] He left his constituency in Stafford for Fox's old seat in Westminster; lost that the following year, 1807, but sat for Ilchester, probably through the influence of the prince regent,

[4] See Sir Lewis Namier and John Brooke, *The History of Parliament: The House of Commons 1754—1790* (London, 1964), III, the best short account of Sheridan's parliamentary career until 1800.

[5] Sir Gilbert Elliott, quoted in R. C. Rhodes, *Harlequin Sheridan* (Oxford, 1933), p. 146

[6] *Letters*, ed. cit., II, nos. 232, 317, 444, and 406.

[7] ibid., nos. 500 and 567.

until 1812, when he again contested the Stafford seat, and lost it. These elections, and his son's unsuccessful contests for Stafford, had cost him a great deal—£20,000 even by 1806, he claimed[8]—and when no longer an MP, he was liable to arrest for debt.[9] In 1809 the Drury Lane theatre had burned down, insured for only a fraction of its value. Sheridan watched the blaze with equanimity from a tavern, saying 'A man may surely take a glass of wine by his own fireside', but he was allowed no part in the control of the theatre once it reopened, and he could no longer draw on its funds for his own use.

His last years were miserable. 'I have never done a dishonest or a base act', he wrote to his wife in 1814,

> I never have omitted to do a generous or a benevolent one where I had the Power—but sins of *omission*—Oh me—senseless credulity, destructive procrastination, unworthy indolence, all abetted by one vile habit . . . [his drinking][10]

He is said to have pawned his books,[11] and a sale of his furniture to pay his creditors was advertised as he lay dying, 'absolutely undone and broken-hearted'.[12] Thomas Moore, his first biographer, inveighs against the 'array of rank' who had neglected the dying man and yet attended his funeral.[13]

## THE PLAY

The first performance of *The Rivals,* on 17 January 1775, was a failure. It had been written in haste, although Sheridan profited (as he acknowledges in the Preface) from the help of Thomas Harris, the manager of Covent Garden, who did not usually involve himself closely in productions.[14] The play itself was too long; the plot and the characters were condemned as improbable and unnatural; and the language censured—'The author seems to have considered puns, witticisms, similes and metaphors, as admirable substitutes for polished diction'.[15] The audience was

[8] ibid., no. 567.

[9] He is said to have been arrested for debt four times: *Letters,* III, no. 853.

[10] ibid., no. 881.

[11] Thomas Moore, *Memoirs of the Life of Sheridan* (3rd ed., London, 1825), II, 441.

[12] *Letters,* III, no. 934.

[13] He died on 7 July 1816. Moore, op. cit., III, 461.

[14] See *Tne London Stage 1660—1800,* Part IV, *1747—1776,* ed. G. W. Stone, Jr (Carbondale, Illinois, 1962), III, 1830.

[15] *Public Ledger,* 18 January 1775, quoted in *The Dramatic Works of Richard Brinsley Sheridan,* ed. Cecil Price (Oxford, 1973), I, 44.

displeased with the robustness of the humour (Restoration plays had to be bowdlerized for the later eighteenth century), and with the character of Sir Lucius, 'so ungenerous an attack upon a nation . . . so villainous a portrait of an Irish Gentleman'.[16] The parts of Sir Lucius and Sir Anthony were, moreover, badly performed: in the fifth act an apple thrown from the audience hit Lee, who played Sir Lucius:

> he stepped forward, and with a genuine rich brogue, angrily cried out, 'By the pow'rs, is it *personal*?—is it me, or the matter?'[17]

It may have been that extra-literary factors, which had aroused interest in the play before its performance, contributed also to its failure. The play is set in Bath, and includes rumours of an elopement and a duel between contestants for the hand of a young lady: Elizabeth Linley and her unwanted suitors had already figured on the stage in Samuel Foote's play *The Maid of Bath* (1771), and Sheridan's two duels with Thomas Mathews, one of the suitors, were public knowledge. The claque to which Sheridan alludes in the Preface (76–86) may have been formed by friends of Mathews, or even, perhaps, by a playwright disappointed that his play had been passed over by the management in favour of a young and untried author's. One contemporary report suggested that 'the literary plunderers, and sentimental blockheads' had tried to hiss it down because it was a farcical, 'laughing' comedy.[18] (This opposition of 'laughing' and sentimental comedy will be discussed below.)

For various reasons, then, the play was withdrawn (it was advertised for the following night, but it is unlikely that any performance took place). Eleven days later, on 28 January, revised, and with another actor as Sir Lucius, it was performed to greater, if still qualified, applause—a work of promise rather than a masterpiece. It had another thirteen performances that season (nine was regarded as a respectable run for a new play). Between 1775 and 1800, it was performed about a hundred times in London, often for benefit performances, which indicates that it was good box office. The most popular play of that period, for comparison, was Sheridan's *The School for Scandal,* which had 261 performances. *The Rivals* seems to have been a particular favourite with the royal family—it had five command performances in ten years—and it

[16] 'A Briton' in the *Morning Post,* 21 January 1775, quoted ibid., I, 47.

[17] See Allardyce Nicoll, *A History of English Drama 1660–1900,* III (Cambridge, 1952), 6.

[18] *Morning Post,* 31 January 1775, quoted in *The Rivals,* ed. from the Larpent manuscript by R. L. Purdy (Oxford, 1935), xii.

was also popular in the provinces.[19] It has held its place in the repertory of the British and American theatre ever since.

The first published text, then, is that of the version which succeeded at the second performance, but a copy of the text for the first performance, submitted to the office of the Lord Chamberlain (who until 1968 censored all new plays), has survived. A comparison of this, the Larpent manuscript, with the first edition, shows how the revisions were effected.[20] The most important changes are in the character of Sir Lucius: in the Larpent version it is suggested by Lucy that he cares little whether he marries Mrs Malaprop or Lydia, as long as he gets the money; he is meaner, and more stupid. He is also more bloodthirsty—'Put him to death', he urges Acres in III.iv—and less punctilious about the finer points of duelling. In the first edition, a more convincing reason is given for his duel with Absolute—an imagined slight made by Absolute on Ireland—and this necessitates some plot changes, in the carrying of the challenge. The means by which Absolute learns that Lydia is the bride his father proposes for him are also changed, and a romance between Fag and Lucy excised, so that they no longer appear in the last scene. Word blunders by characters other than Mrs Malaprop are also removed, apart from Sir Lucius's 'bulls'. In all, seventeen scenes are reduced to fourteen.

The changes in tone are the most interesting. Many of the *double entendres* are removed; in IV.iii, for instance, it is much more obvious in the Larpent manuscript that Jack is suspected of upsetting Lydia by making crude advances to her—'Rogue, couldn't you wait for the parson', asks Sir Anthony. Jack's attitude to Lydia is rather more cynical, and even Faulkland is given a 'man of the world' speech. Sir Anthony is more outspoken in the Larpent version—he chides Jack, in III.i, on his seeming lack of enthusiasm for the marriage, that he will 'lie like a cucumber, on a hot bed'—and he is also more violent in his temper. Various of Sir Lucius's and Mrs Malaprop's speeches are cleaned up, and one malapropism, 'salivation' (V.i, 184), which could refer to the mercury treatment for venereal disease, and which managed to survive the first revision, was changed in the third edition of 1776.

There were, however, additions as well as excisions. R. L. Purdy, who calculated that the text of the first edition is only 500 words shorter than that of the Larpent version, argued that these additional 'flowers of rhetoric blossom most abundantly in the Julia–Faulkland scenes', although some were again removed in the

[19] These figures are taken from *The London Stage,* Part IV, and Part V, ed. C. B. Hogan (Carbondale, Illinois, 1968).

[20] See R. L Purdy's very useful edition.

third edition.[21] Many audiences, readers, and directors might indeed be happier if the Julia–Faulkland episodes were cut even more, as they have been in many productions.[22]

It is usually thought that the problem with the Julia–Faulkland subplot is its sentimentality, which fits ill with the more farcically comic mood of the rest of the play. This opposition between 'laughing' and sentimental comedy has to be elucidated to put *The Rivals* into its context in the later eighteenth-century theatre. As we have seen, the changes made for the second performance were to accommodate an audience which in 1775 was much more fastidious about sexual innuendo than it had been in the earlier eighteenth century. Sheridan's revision of Vanbrugh's *The Relapse* (as *A Trip to Scarborough,* 1777) shows this tendency clearly. This dislike of bawdry had not been a sudden development, and it is linked with the growing popularity of more moral and sentimental plays.

It used to be thought that by the 1770s the staple fare on the London stage was sentimental comedies, in which much emphasis was put on long-drawn-out scenes of pathos, hairbreadth escapes from ruin (financial or moral), recognition of long-lost children, and similarly emotive discoveries. Certainly there were such comedies, and some contemporaries thought they were too popular—Goldsmith, for instance, whose essay on comedy will be discussed below, and Sheridan himself, as witness the Preface to *The Rivals* and the Prologue on the Tenth Night—but these plays were only part of a varied repertoire.[23] In the 1760s and 1770s, only about a sixth of the new plays could be described as sentimental comedies,[24] although some were egregiously sentimental. In Arthur Murphy's *The Grecian Daughter,* for instance, Euphrasia saves her father, who has been sentenced to die by starvation, by suckling him secretly. In the last week of February 1772, *The Grecian Daughter* was performed three times at Drury Lane, but another nine plays were put on that week. These were two sentimental comedies (Cumberland's *The West Indian* and Colman's *The English Merchant*), three 'laughing' comedies (Murphy's *The Way to Keep Him,* Farquhar's *The Inconstant,* and Colman's *The*

[21] ibid., p.xli.

[22] See M. S. Auburn, 'The Pleasures of Sheridan's *The Rivals*', *Modern Philology* LXXII (1975), 260 and 265.

[23] See Arthur Sherbo, *English Sentimental Drama* (East Lansing, Michigan, 1957) and R. D. Hume, 'Goldsmith and Sheridan and the supposed Revolution of "Laughing" against "Sentimental" Comedy', in P. J. Korshin, ed., *Studies in Change and Revolution* (Menston, Yorkshire, 1972), pp. 237–76.

[24] See ibid., pp. 252–7.

*Jealous Wife*), a tragedy, *Barbarossa,* by John Brown, a 'mawkish' comic opera, Bickerstaffe's *The Maid of the Mill, Much Ado about Nothing,* and *Romeo and Juliet.*[25] So, of a total of twelve performances at the two theatres, six (if we include *The Maid of the Mill*) were of sentimental comedy, four of 'laughing' comedy, and two of tragedy. Since *The Grecian Daughter* had three performances in its first week, the balance of sentimental comedy is probably greater than usual.

It must be remembered that any sentimental play also competed in mood with *entr'actes* and an afterpiece, since the five-act play composed only part of the evening's entertainment. Singing, dancing, or comic interludes took place between the acts of the mainpiece—at one performance of *The Grecian Daughter* the play was followed by an actor delivering 'a humorous address . . . from the back of a pantomine rhinoceros'.[26] The afterpiece might be a short farce, a ballad opera, a burlesque, or a pantomime, and farces were especially popular in the last half of the eighteenth century.[27] In considering the later eighteenth-century theatre as a whole, we must not underestimate the importance of these afterpieces:

> The number of non-traditional, comic-type plays written and produced increased with each season; by 1776 they constituted the largest single bloc of performances in the repertoire, dominating everything else—tragedy, laughing and sentimental comedy, farce.[28]

Thus, not only was the weekly repertoire of mainpieces varied, but each evening's entertainment also offered variations in mood—*King Lear*, for instance, might be followed by *Catherine and Petruchio*, a farcically abbreviated version of *The Taming of the Shrew* by Garrick.[29]

Although scholars have thus corrected the mistaken idea that sentimental comedy was dominant in the later eighteenth century, we have nevertheless to acknowledge that Goldsmith and Sheridan, the playwrights we consider the most important in the period, both censured the popularity of such plays. In 1773 Goldsmith wrote an article attacking the 'Weeping Sentimental Comedy, so

[25] See *The London Stage,* Part IV. The classification of the plays is taken from Nicoll, op. cit.

[26] See *The London Stage,* Part IV, III, for 5 May 1774, and *The Revels History of Drama in English,* VI, *1750–1880* (London, 1975), Robertson Davies, 'Playwrights and Plays', 168.

[27] See *The London Stage,* Part IV, I, cxlv.

[28] *Eighteenth Century Drama: Afterpieces,* ed. R. W. Bevis (London, 1970), p. xii.

[29] *The London Stage,* Part IV, III, for 23 March 1776.

much in fashion at present', in which 'the Distresses, rather than the Faults of Mankind, make our interest in the piece'.[30] He implies, therefore, that one function of comedy is to correct folly by ridiculing it, and in this respect both Goldsmith's own plays and *The Rivals* might be said to be un-sentimental (Lydia's romantic delusions and Acres's pretensions to fashion, for instance, are clearly ridiculed). Goldsmith also argues that sentiment is somehow more fitted to a feebler sort of writing, like novels: 'Those abilities that can hammer out a Novel, are fully sufficient for the production of a Sentimental Comedy', and Sheridan follows him in this.[31] But Goldsmith's attack on sentimental comedy can be taken too generally: part of his argument relies on the snobbish appeal that plays about tradesmen are not interesting (although sentimental comedies most often used upper-class characters),[32] and one of his main purposes in the article was to arouse interest in his own forthcoming play, *She Stoops to Conquer,* which, like *The Rivals,* is a 'laughing' and even farcical comedy.[33] Both Goldsmith and Sheridan, then, attack sentimental comedy, and present their own plays as returning to the true vein of 'laughing' comedy. Yet both are to some extent affected by the changes in taste which had made sentimental comedy possible, and popular: their 'laughing' comedies are genial, not satiric; they avoid the presentation of lust or cruelty and other baser facets of human nature; and they move to a clear and cheerful resolution in which everyone has some cause for rejoicing.[34] As we have seen, the first version of *The Rivals* in the Larpent manuscript conforms less to this pattern than the final one.

Here we return to the problem of the Julia–Faulkland episodes. Are their long, sentimental speeches and finely wrought emotions a sop to the taste of the audience, or a satire on the misdirection of that taste to sentimental comedy? John Bernard, an actor and writer of the period, argued in his *Retrospections* that Sheridan designed Julia and Faulkland merely to cater to the audience, whose taste was so vitiated that they were preferred to the more

[30] 'An Essay on the Theatre; or, A Comparison between Laughing and Sentimental Comedy' (1773), in *Collected Works,* ed. Arthur Friedman (Oxford, 1966), III, 212.

[31] ibid., 213.

[32] ibid., 212–13: see Sherbo, op. cit., p. 132.

[33] See Hume, op. cit., p. 238: several of the actors and actresses in *The Rivals* had played similar parts in *She Stoops to Conquer.*

[34] See John Loftis, *Sheridan and the Drama of Georgian England* (Oxford, 1976), pp. 10 and 31.

comic characters.[35] Contemporary notices of the play, however, vary:

> Falkland is a great proof of heart-felt delicacy . . . the exquisite refinement in his disposition, opposed to the noble simplicity, tenderness, and candor of Julia's, give rise to some of the most affecting sentimental scenes I ever remember to have met with.
>
> Few of the characters are new, and scarce any well supported: those of Falkland and Miss Melville are the most *outré* sentimental ones that ever appeared upon the stage.[36]

This diversity of response is a salutary reminder to the literary student that the 'eighteenth-century audience' is no more monolithic or unvarying in its views than any modern audience, and that a play is much more than its text. In later productions, changes in taste can be gauged by the different emphases put on Faulkland's part; on the American stage, for instance,

> in 1829, brilliant acting is needed to portray the captious sceptic in love; in 1864, his part is relegated to the closet and 'high comedy'; and in 1913, he has once again become interesting, this time by virtue of his originality and individuality.[37]

In recent productions, the part has been carried only with difficulty, and provokes more laughter than sympathetic indulgence in the audience. It seems clear, however, that in 1775 Faulkland was played seriously, and with care.

Even so, the sentimentality is qualified. Faulkland is not wildly generous, a salient characteristic of sentimental heroes ('they are lavish enough of their *Tin* Money on the Stage', complained Goldsmith).[38] He recognizes his faults, which are condemned by Absolute as well as by Julia, and which are punished in her rejection of him (although the comic structure is preserved in their final reconciliation). In this respect, Faulkland is less of a sentimental hero than Charles in *The School for Scandal.*

Julia acts as a foil to Faulkland's captious sentimentality, and to Lydia's romantic attitudes, and is faulty less for being sentimental than for seeming priggish. Her speech concluding the play, which might well be viewed as sentimental, is rather a stock device, the

[35] *Retrospections of the Stage* (London, 1830), I, 142–6, quoted in *The Dramatic Works,* ed. cit., I, 54–5.

[36] 'One of the Pit', in the *Morning Chronicle,* 27 January 1775, and *The Town and Country Magazine,* VII (1775), 43, both quoted in *The Dramatic Works,* ed. cit., I, 47 and 45.

[37] Auburn, op. cit., 264.

[38] 'An Essay on the Theatre', ed. cit., III, 212.

'tag'. The end of a play was often signalled, not only by the resolution of the plot, but visibly, by the actors' lining up to face the audience (V.iii, 257. 'The rest come forward'). The actor or actress who was to speak the tag would step forward, out of line, so that the speech was in a sense marked off from the play, and it was usually, as in *The Rivals,* moralistic and generalizing.[39]

*The Rivals* follows convention in many more ways than in having a tag. Despite Sheridan's disclaimer in the Preface that he knew little of plays or the theatre, the play's success rests partly on its being such a combination of theatrical stereotypes. Much time and effort has been expended in discovering antecedents and models for various of the characters. Mrs Malaprop probably leads the field. It is not only that word blunders are a stock source of comic relief—in Shakespeare there are, among others, Dogberry, Mistress Quickly, and Launcelot Gobbo—but that women who make these blunders abound in the eighteenth century, in novels (Mrs Slipslop in *Joseph Andrews,* Tabitha Bramble and Win Jenkins in *Humphrey Clinker,* for instance) as well as in plays.[40] In 1766, Garrick had commented on a play sent for his approval

> *Civil* is like too many Chambermaids of lat[e] who mistake Words, and I think that humour very near Exhausted.[41]

Lydia is neither the first nor the last young person shown to be deluded by novel reading:

> My Father, seduced by the false glare of Fortune and the Deluding Pomp of Title, insisted on my giving my hand to Lady Dorothea. No never exclaimed I. Lady Dorothea is lovely and Engaging; I prefer no woman to her; but know Sir, that I scorn to marry her in Compliance with your Wishes. No! Never shall it be said that I Obliged my Father. 'Where, Edward in the name of wonder (said he) did you pick up this unmeaning gibberish? You have been studying Novels I suspect'. I scorned to answer: it would have been beneath my dignity.[42]

Faulkland's name may be taken from Sheridan's mother's novel,

[39] See *London Stage,* Part V, I, lxxxix.

[40] See Loftis, op. cit., 48–50: S. K. Sen, 'Sheridan's Literary Debt to *Humphrey Clinker*', *Modern Language Quarterly,* XXI (1960): the list of plays with similar characters includes Colman and Garrick's *The Clandestine Marriage* (1766), Garrick's *Lethe* (1740), Arthur Murphy's *The Upholsterer* (1758), and Frances Sheridan's unfinished play, *A Journey to Bath.*

[41] *The Letters of David Garrick,* eds D. M. Little and G. M. Kahrl (London, 1963), II, no. 422.

[42] Jane Austen, *Works*, ed. R. W. Chapman (London, 1963), VI, 81 ('Love and Freindship', Letter 6th): cf. also George Colman's 'dramatic novel' *Polly Honeycombe* (1760), and Charlotte Lennox, *The Female Quixote* (1752).

his character from other plays,[43] and Acres, as the amiable bumpkin who tries to be sophisticated, is a descendant of a long line which some commentators date from Sir Andrew Aguecheek in *Twelfth Night,* and which surely includes Tony Lumpkin in *She Stoops to Conquer* (the parts were played by the same actor at their first performances).[44] The heavy father and the pert maid are so common that no specific models need be sought, and Sir Lucius is completely the stage Irishman of the eighteenth century, amorous and pugnacious, a perfect example of the type.[45]

Whole scenes and situations echo those in previous works. In Steele's *The Tender Husband* (1705), the heroine is determined to act as if she were in a romance, and her lover indulges her in this for his own ends: the father of one of her suitors, like Sir Anthony, boasts of his severity to his son—'I have never suffered him to have anything he liked in his life'.[46] When Jack Absolute agrees to marry to his father's liking, knowing that the bride is his own choice, the scene is almost a parody of one in Steele's later play, *The Conscious Lovers* (1722), in which the priggish hero agrees that he will marry the woman his father has chosen.[47] There are other parallels with two of Congreve's plays, *The Way of the World* and *Love for Love,* with the Bath scenes in Smollett's novel *Humphrey Clinker,* and with Sheridan's mother's work, especially her unfinished play *A Journey to Bath.*[48] To point out these similarities does not, of course, imply that Sheridan was consciously using these works, but it does emphasize the stock nature of the characters and situations in *The Rivals.*

It is therefore not surprising that the structure of the play can be seen as conforming to one of the models of comedy put forward by Northrop Frye in his *Anatomy of Criticism.*[49] The love-affair be-

[43] See Alicia Lefanu, *Memoirs of the Life and Writings of Mrs Frances Sheridan* (London, 1824), p. 115: and Tuvia Block, 'The Antecedents of Sheridan's Faulkland', *Philological Quarterly* XLIX (1970), 266–8.

[44] Hazlitt mentions Sir Andrew Aguecheek in *Lectures on the English Comic Writers,* in *Complete Works,* ed. P. P. Howe (London and Toronto, 1931), VI, 165: see also M. E. Knapp, *Prologues and Epilogues of the Eighteenth Century* (Yale Studies in English 149, New Haven, 1961), p. 90: and J. H. Smith, 'Tony Lumpkin and the Country Booby type in antecedent English comedy', *PMLA* LVIII (1943), 1038–49.

[45] See J. O. Bartley, 'The Development of a Stock Character', *Modern Language Review* XXXVII (1942), 438–47, and *Teague, Shenkin and Sawney* (Cork, 1954), pp. 167–90.

[46] *The Tender Husband,* ed. Calhoun Winter (London, 1967), I, l. 295.

[47] *The Conscious Lovers,* ed. S. S. Kenny (London, 1968), I, ii.

[48] See Loftis, op. cit., pp. 48–50; and Sen, op. cit.

[49] *Anatomy of Criticism* (Princeton, New Jersey, 1957), especially pp. 164–74.

tween Absolute and Lydia is impeded by two older, 'blocking' characters, figures of authority who are both ridiculous—Sir Anthony because of his temper, Mrs Malaprop for her word blunders. They not only deceive themselves (Sir Anthony thinks he is a lenient father, Mrs Malaprop thinks herself 'queen of the dictionary') but are also deceived by the plot: the marriage which they want to bring about for prudent, financial reasons has already been decided on by the young people. Their authority is thus undermined, since although they imagine themselves to be directing the behaviour of Lydia and Jack, they are in fact acquiescing in a decision already made on the basis not of prudent calculation but of love and sexual attraction (although Jack, but not Lydia, combines love with prudence).

In the 'discovery' scene (IV.ii), however, the plot is complicated by Lydia's rejection of Jack now that he is no longer romantically penniless. Lydia herself now becomes a 'blocking' character, and she is well fitted for that role, since she, like Sir Anthony and Mrs Malaprop, is conceived in terms of a 'humour', or typifying characteristic—her addiction to novel-reading and the false ideals which that imposes on her view of the world. Thus Lydia is also a ridiculous and absurd character, imprisoned (as it were) in her false perception of what love is, and she cannot escape from this bondage until the reconciliations of the last scene. It matters little that she is inconsistent in then abandoning her desire for a picturesque elopement, although the action is made probable enough by her fear for Jack's life in the duel.

Jack, by contrast, is a more straightforward hero: handsome, courageous, and not too much in love to be unmanly and ridiculous, or to forget that financial comfort is desirable. He exemplifies Byron's dictum:

> Man's love is of man's life a thing apart,
> 'Tis woman's whole existence.

He is able to manipulate not only the authority figures (he tricks Sir Anthony and Mrs Malaprop) but also Lydia, at least before IV.ii, and it is as well that he is worsted by her then, since it not only increases our interest in the plot (how will this complication be resolved, since we know all will end happily?), but also makes Jack more likeable than if he were always in control.

And of course he is not. It is Sir Anthony's sudden irruption upon Bath that sets the play going, and Jack has little control over Acres and Sir Lucius, his compeers and rivals for Lydia's love. Both are hopeless candidates, no more capable of winning the fair lady than any other clown figure, and their function in the plot is to provide laughs and multiply complications, in both of which they succeed. Acres is more sympathetically treated than is the country bumpkin in Restoration comedy; he is not in any way cruel or destructive, and even in the duel, although we laugh at his cowardice, we are more in sympathy with his view of it than with Sir Lucius's (and so, it is likely, the audience of 1775 would have been). The duel scene is treated comically, even farcically, rather than sentimentally; there is no didactic sermon against duelling as in *The Conscious Lovers.*[50] And if we sometimes laugh with Acres, we laugh more *at* him, at his affectation of fashion, and his shirking from a bullet in the vitals. There is no suggestion that he be allowed any love interest (as, for instance, Charlie Chaplin, a much more sentimental clown, sometimes is).

Sir Lucius is rather a more dangerous figure, in terms of the comic structure. In the Larpent version, since he was more bloodthirsty, his discomfiture in the final scene was more cruel, and his reconciliation into the final harmony therefore more crude. In the play as we have it, however, the edge is taken off his character, and his gentlemanly behaviour in the last scene makes Mrs Malaprop the more ridiculous. Since Lucy, the agent of the deception, is not present, the emphasis falls on Sir Lucius's taking it all in good part, and the conflict of the title is resolved in a party to be given by one of the 'losers'. Yet no one has really 'lost': and to that extent *The Rivals* is more sentimental than comedies where a villain cannot be brought into the circle of harmony (as in *The Tempest,* or *Much Ado about Nothing*), or where even a character who has erred rather than plotted is excluded (as in *The Way of the World*). The ending of *The Rivals* fulfils expectations rather than offers complexities.

It is not therefore to be condemned, and its sentimentality, as I have argued, is kept within bounds. Since Julia and Faulkland provide the sub-plot,[51] our interest in their affair is the less. The captiousness which characterizes Faulkland's sensibility is indeed an aspect of sentimentality often satirized in the later eighteenth century, but it is not confined to that period. Johnson defines it as 'Inclination to find fault . . . peevishness' and cites Locke's condemnation,

> *Captiousness* is a fault opposite to civility; it often produces misbecoming and provoking expressions and carriage,[52]

which would go far to summing up Faulkland.

[50] See ed. cit., Preface, p. 5.

[51] cf. ibid., pp. xvii and xxv.

[52] Samuel Johnson, *A Dictionary of the English Language* (4th ed., London, 1773), sv 'Captiousness'.

In some ways the problem with the Julia–Faulkland sub-plot is less its sentimentality than its lack of integration. Their affair has little to do with the complications of the plot, since there is no external obstacle to their marriage. Julia is as much a problem as Faulkland: like Jack, she is more 'ordinary' than the other characters, but unlike him, she is unable to direct any of the action, and thus appears too passive, and too exemplary.

Yet the sub-plot is not entirely divorced from the action of the play. There are obvious parallels between the pairs of lovers; Julia and Jack are sensible and 'ordinary', Lydia and Faulkland absurd because deluded (although Faulkland's more psychologically convincing delusion is out of key with the tone of the rest of the play).[53] Both men test the strength of the women's love by deceiving them, and both women resent it enough to break off the affair for a time. The matches are both realistic in that they are between young people of comparable social standing and attractiveness, not January linked to May, which tends to a satiric treatment, or the prince and the beggar maid, which is the stuff of romance. In that sense *The Rivals* is set firmly in a world where financial considerations are important in marriage, although love is also necessary (as in Jane Austen). Lydia's willingness to marry a penniless ensign is silly; and although Julia will follow Faulkland into exile, she contemplates a lack of splendour rather than bare poverty.

There is a clear differentiation in the play between the language of sentiment and affectation and the language of normal life. Faulkland generally speaks in the language of sentiment. He amplifies and heightens his emotions, and he uses poetic language and constructions. Julia shares this language in their scenes together: it is characterized by the use both of exclamations (to represent the abrupt force of their feelings), and of more complex syntactical constructions which demonstrate their ability to discriminate finely (their feelings are exquisite and delicate):

FAULKLAND
O Julia! I am bankrupt in gratitude! but the time is so pressing, it calls on you for so hasty a resolution. Would you not wish some hours to weigh the advantages you forego, and what little compensation poor Faulkland can make you beside his solitary love?

JULIA
I ask not a moment. No, Faulkland, I have loved you for yourself: and if I now, more than ever, prize the solemn engagement which so long has pledged us to each other, it is because it leaves no room for hard aspersions on my fame, and puts the seal of duty to an act of love. But let us not linger—perhaps this delay—— (V.i, 30–40)

[53] cf. Loftis, op. cit., pp. 52–3.

Julia is, however, less exclamatory and more reasonable. Her defence of Faulkland to Lydia (I.ii) is a model of antithetical construction and of qualification (one critic has called it 'computer-like').[54] She cannot but appear too sensible to be interesting when her judgement clearly moulds the form of her speech, balancing one possibility against another, as in her final forgiveness of Faulkland.

Lydia uses some of the same poetic language, but always more passionately. It is clear that her sensibility is an assumed role, since she can also be witty, and her romantic language is, of course, burlesqued. It is also clear when Jack adopts the 'man of feeling' role that he has some motive for doing so, to deceive his father, Mrs Malaprop, or Lydia, and the audience is left in no doubt that his language is assumed. Lydia and Mrs Malaprop are taken in by it, but Sir Anthony is less susceptible:

> ABSOLUTE
> Pardon me, Sir, I never saw you look more strong and hearty; and I pray frequently that you may continue so.
> SIR ANTHONY
> I hope your prayers may be heard with all my heart. Well then, Jack, I have been considering that I am so strong and hearty, I may continue to plague you a long time. (II.i, 338–42)

Indeed, Sir Anthony can himself consciously affect the language of sentiment, in comic contrast with his more usual tone, blunt even when he is not roused to anger:

> Here we are, Mrs Malaprop; come to mitigate the frowns of unrelenting beauty—and difficulty enough I had to bring this fellow. I don't know what's the matter; but if I hadn't held him by force, he'd have given me the slip. (IV.ii, 29–32)

Mrs Malaprop blunders into sentimental language when describing her feelings for her late husband, but her malapropisms show her desire to be thought intellectual, since she misuses the terms of science (in its wider eighteenth-century sense of knowledge acquired by study).

Such linguistic contrasts are to be expected in a play which works by setting one attitude (exemplified in a character) against another; where Sir Lucius's calm civility is compared, for instance, with Acres's belligerence in writing the challenge. We laugh at the incongruity, which functions in the contrast not only of two characters, but also in that between a character's view of himself or

[54] Allan Rodway, 'Goldsmith and Sheridan: Satirists of Sentiment', in *Renaissance and Modern Essays,* ed. G. R. Hibbard (London, 1966), p. 70.

herself and the judgement that others (including the audience) are enabled to make. Mrs Malaprop's blunders are an obvious example, and Acres's attempts at gentility and 'polish'. They are made comical by their language, although Acres certainly and Mrs Malaprop very probably are also visually ridiculous. They are neatly distinguished in that his affectation is social success, hers intellectual prowess (although she also suffers discomfiture in love).

Mrs Malaprop blunders not through ignorance but through misapplied and jumbled knowledge, notably of the physical sciences and of grammar, almost in a monstrous parody of Dr Johnson's attempt to extend the range of the language by introducing scientific and technical terms in metaphorical senses. Sometimes she does hit a surprisingly appropriate note (although not the right note), as when she chides Sir Anthony for speaking 'laconically', or when she calls Sir Lucius a 'barbarous Vandyke', the dark handsome cavalier of her idealization of him. She can speak truer than she knows: boarding-school misses might well learn 'ingenuity and artifice', and her own language is very much 'oracular'. Mrs Malaprop's errors conform to no set formula—she produces 'bulls' as well as mistaking words—but her most memorable lines are those where she does achieve a wild and flurrying appropriateness, in calling Jack the 'pineapple of perfection', for instance, or Lydia 'headstrong as an allegory' and then compounding her error (and our delight) by adding 'on the banks of Nile'.

Mrs Malaprop is the quintessential, and proverbial, character in a play where all the characters but Julia provide comic revelations in their language. Jack consciously adopts the sentimental mode, and Lucy is similarly self-conscious. The other revelations—Lydia, Faulkland, and Sir Anthony have already been discussed—are involuntary. Sir Lucius conforms to the Irish stereotype in making 'bulls'; David involves himself in trains of misassociations: Fag affects the language of a gentleman (as well as betraying the shallowness of his sensibility by beating the kitchen boy).

That the language of *The Rivals* is so marked, so defamiliarized, tells us something more about the play. It is a combination of theatrical stereotypes, with a plot structure conforming almost to a pattern of comedy, but its success lies in this very stereotyping. Our pleasure in the design of *The Rivals* is parallel to our pleasure in its humours characters, since it springs from the principle of repetition as a comic force, what Frye has called 'the literary imitation of ritual bondage'.[55] The characters and situations are not

[55] op. cit., p. 168.

only typical, but pushed to the extreme which makes them burlesque, so that our delight in them is not in seeing how much they resemble life but in the fulfilment of expectation to the uttermost degree, and self-consciously so.[56] *The Rivals* does not function entirely as burlesque, but many of its best scenes—Absolute and his father, Mrs Malaprop overhearing Absolute and Lydia, Acres and David—rely on this principle of imitation which works by excess. Of course the play and its characters are not entirely fantastic: eighteenth-century fathers might well be authoritarian and concerned to marry their sons to a fortune rather than take account of the sons' choice. But this would not explain our delight in Sir Anthony; it is rather the way in which he overtops expectation, in being the quintessence of the authoritarian father (and at the same time ridiculous), that makes him a good character.

This was not the reaction of the first audiences, who wanted characters to be 'natural'. In his *Retrospections,* Bernard singled out Mrs Malaprop, now probably thought its most memorable personage, as the single most important reason for 'the partial failure of the play'.[57] The eighteenth-century audience might also have seen the play as more 'natural' in the possibility that it caught references to Sheridan's courtship of Elizabeth Linley, and his duels with Mathews, which have already been mentioned. Later, the tutor of Sheridan's son was to point out resemblances between the author and the character of Faulkland:

> . . . I was at no loss to discern where he had found the character of Faulkland, and I could easily comprehend all that Mrs Canning told me of the sufferings of Mrs Sheridan, who was destined, this moment to adore the man for his affection and brilliant talents, whom she was the next moment to be ready to detest and fly from, overpowered and indignant at his teazing unreasonableness and nervous, unintelligible folly.[58]

As John Loftis comments on the autobiographical aspects of the play,

> the half-submerged allusions to episodes known to his audience . . . represent a subtle and tactful means of making capital out of personal celebrity.[59]

For us, however, these references are more a revelation of how life strives to resemble art, and the Bath setting has merely a period

[56] cf. Loftis, op. cit., pp. 3–6.
[57] ed. cit., p. 54.
[58] William Smyth, *Memoir of Mr Sheridan* (Leeds, 1840), pp. 7–8, quoted Purdy, op. cit., p. xliv.
[59] Loftis, op. cit., p. 56.

flavour. Bath is, nevertheless, important to the play. It is an artificial environment: a resort where miscellaneous visitors gathered, ostensibly to restore their health by drinking the waters,but often for other purposes—to enjoy the balls, the assemblies, the garden walks and the fine modern architecture, the delights of circulating libraries and print shops, hairdressers, tailors, milliners, and dancing masters, in a word fashion and conspicuous consumption. The country bumpkin with money could there acquire 'polish', like Acres or Simkin Blunderhead in the popular contemporary poem *The New Bath Guide.*[60] The penniless dandy might acquire a rich wife, as Sir Lucius tries to, or like Sir Ulic Mackilligut, the Irish knight in *Humphrey Clinker* who is taking dancing lessons at the age of sixty, and who tries to captivate the middle-aged Tabitha Bramble. Bath society was less exclusive than London: there the country gentry might mingle with a larger and more interesting group of acquaintance than their often quite isolated rural neighbourhoods afforded: their daughters could meet eligible young men (or unsuitable penniless ensigns). Bath provided both opportunity and temptation: young women might be ruined as well as suitably married, young gentlemen lose fortunes at gambling.

The ambience of Bath is perfect for *The Rivals*—a world of enjoyment and intrigue, fashionable, and unaffected by humdrum cares. It is artificial, and this artificiality and staginess in the play have been much condemned:

> its dependence on formula, contrivance, tips to the audience, plot summaries, scene-shifting and stage business, playable circumstances and playable characters at the expense of consistency and subtlety, the comfortable simplifying echo of dead authors' perceptions—all the paraphernalia of the well-made popular play of any age.[61]

It is true that *The Rivals* does not offer us 'high seriousness' or a 'criticism of life'. If it is a fault to be popular, then *The Rivals* is greatly to be condemned, for it has been one of the most frequently performed plays of the eighteenth century, and has been revived, for instance, five times in the past couple of years.[62] In that it is stagey, it works far better on the stage than in the study, and offers a number of good parts and the possibility of an interesting

[60] See Christopher Anstey, *The New Bath Guide* (9th ed., London, 1773), Letter X.

[61] Marvin Mudrick, 'Restoration Comedy and Later', in *English Stage Comedy,* ed. W. K. Wimsatt (New York, 1955), p. 116: cf. A. N. Kaul, *The Action of English Comedy* (New Haven and London, 1970), pp. 131–49.

[62] By the Royal Exchange company (Manchester), 1976; Theatr Clwyd (Mold), 1978; Southern Exchange (Swindon), 1978; the Crucible Theatre (Sheffield), 1977; and the Prospect Theatre company (at the Old Vic, London), 1978.

design, since it needs the full paraphernalia of the theatre. No one would argue that it has no faults: the plot is static and the action to some extent predictable, since the play works, not by revealing character, but by displaying it. We know that the lovers will win over the curmudgeons, and we are interested less in how this is brought about than in the opportunities afforded for the curmudgeons to be pompous, tyrannical, and silly, and for the lovers to be lover-like (and also silly). Thus the play is locally effective, but poor on continuity: individual scenes (as those between Absolute and his father) work very well, but they are in the nature of set pieces, and the concatenation of scenes is weak. The dialogue is witty, but there is no subtlety of character revelation. If we compare Mrs Malaprop with one of her illustrious forebears, Dogberry, a much less important character in *Much Ado* than she is in *The Rivals,* it is clear that her function is much more to display her humour, affectation, than to fulfil any dramatic role in forwarding the plot (and this is one reason why Faulkland's role is problematic, because he forwards his own plot). There is no comparison between Sheridan and Jonson, the greatest English dramatist of humours, and *The Rivals* is more superficial than the best of Restoration comedy. Yet on stage, as Hazlitt pointed out, it 'has the broadest and most palpable effect';[63] it succeeds as burlesque, and profits by the staginess which has been so often criticized.

[63] ed. cit., VI, 165.

## NOTE ON THE TEXT

THE COPY-TEXT for this edition is the Cambridge University Library copy of the first edition (referred to in the notes as 1775). New readings from the third edition (1776) are admitted, and some errors corrected from the fourth edition. For the Prologue and the Prologue on the Tenth Night the copy-text is the third edition. In this the text follows that of Cecil Price's edition of Sheridan (Oxford, 1973), with the difference that spelling and punctuation are modernized throughout. I have occasionally preferred the reading of 1775 where Professor Price has emended it to 1776: these instances are given in the textual notes.

All references to and quotations from Shakespeare are from the *Complete Works,* edited by Peter Alexander (1951).

Other abbreviations follow New Mermaid style: ed. = this and other editors; s.d. = stage direction; *OED* = Oxford English Dictionary.

## FURTHER READING

Auburn, Mark S., 'The Pleasures of Sheridan's *The Rivals:* a Critical Study in the Light of Stage History', *Modern Philology* LXXII (1974–75)

Frye, Northrop, *Anatomy of Criticism* (Princeton, New Jersey, 1957)

Hogan, C. B., *The London Stage* Part V: *1776—1800* (Carbondale, Illinois, 1968)

Hume, R. D., 'Goldsmith and Sheridan and the Supposed Revolution of "Laughing" against "Sentimental" Comedy', in P. J. Korshin, ed., *Studies in Change and Revolution. Aspects of English Intellectual History 1640—1800* (Menston, Yorkshire, 1972)

Loftis, John, *Sheridan and the Drama of Georgian England* (Oxford, 1976)

Price, Cecil, *The Letters of Richard Brinsley Sheridan* (Oxford, 1966)

'The First Prologue to *The Rivals*', *Review of English Studies* n.s. XX (1969)

*The Dramatic Works of Richard Brinsley Sheridan* (Oxford, 1973)

Purdy, R. L., *The Rivals, A Comedy,* edited from the Larpent MS (Oxford, 1935)

Smollett, Tobias, *Humphrey Clinker* (1771), ed. Angus Ross (Harmondsworth, 1967)

Stone, G. W., *The London Stage,* Part IV: *1747—1776* (Carbondale, Illinois, 1962)

I regret that I have not been able to consult Mark S. Auburn, *Sheridan's Comedies: their Contexts and Achievements* (Lincoln, Nebraska, 1978).

# THE RIVALS,

A

# COMEDY.

As it is ACTED at the

Theatre-Royal in Covent-Garden.

---

LONDON:
Printed for JOHN WILKIE, No. 71, St. Paul's Church-Yard.
MDCCLXXV.

## PREFACE

A PREFACE to a play seems generally to be considered as a kind of closet-prologue, in which—if his piece has been successful—the author solicits that indulgence from the reader which he had before experienced from the audience: but as the scope and immediate object of a play is to please a mixed assembly in the representation (whose judgement in the theatre at least is decisive) its degree of reputation is usually as determined as public, before it can be prepared for the cooler tribunal of the study. Thus any further solicitude on the part of the writer becomes unnecessary at least, if not an intrusion: and if the piece has been condemned in the performance, I fear an address to the closet, like an appeal to posterity, is constantly regarded as the procrastination of a suit, from a consciousness of the weakness of the cause. From these considerations, the following comedy would certainly have been submitted to the reader, without any further introduction than what it had in the representation, but that its success has probably been founded on a circumstance which the author is informed has not before attended a theatrical trial, and which consequently ought not to pass unnoticed.

I need scarcely add, that the circumstance alluded to, was the withdrawing of the piece, to remove those imperfections in the first representation which were too obvious to escape reprehension, and too numerous to admit of a hasty correction. There are few writers, I believe, who, even in the fullest consciousness of error, do not wish to palliate the faults which they acknowledge; and, however trifling the performance, to second their confession of its deficiencies, by whatever plea seems least disgraceful to their ability. In the present instance, it cannot be said to amount either to candour or modesty in me, to acknowledge an extreme inexperience and want of judgement on matters, in which, without guidance from practice, or spur from success, a young man should scarcely boast of being an adept. If it be said, that under such disadvantages no one should attempt to write a play—I must beg leave to dissent from the position, while the first point of experience that I have gained on

2 *closet-prologue* the preamble to a play when it is read rather than seen
11 *closet* a private room; hence, the reader
12 *suit* lawsuit
28 *candour* ingenuousness

---

21 *the withdrawing of the piece* see Introduction, p. xiv–xvi

the subject is, a knowledge of the candour and judgement with which an impartial public distinguishes between the errors of inexperience and incapacity, and the indulgence which it shows even to a disposition to remedy the defects of either.

It were unnecessary to enter into any farther extenuation of what was thought exceptionable in this play, but that it has been said, that the managers should have prevented some of the defects before its appearance to the public—and in particular the uncommon length of the piece as represented the first night. It were an ill return for the most liberal and gentlemanly conduct on their side, to suffer any censure to rest where none was deserved. Hurry in writing has long been exploded as an excuse for an author; however, in the dramatic line, it may happen, that both an author and a manager may wish to fill a chasm in the entertainment of the public with a hastiness not altogether culpable. The season was advanced when I first put the play into Mr Harris's hand: it was at that time at least double the length of any acting comedy. I profited by his judgement and experience in the curtailing of it—till, I believe, his feeling for the vanity of a young author got the better of his desire for correctness, and he left many excrescences remaining, because he had assisted in pruning so many more. Hence, though I was not uninformed that the acts were still too long, I flattered myself that, after the first trial, I might with safer judgement proceed to remove what should appear to have been most dissatisfactory. Many other errors there were, which might in part have arisen from my being by no means conversant with plays in general, either in reading or at the theatre. Yet I own that, in one respect, I did not regret my ignorance: for as my first wish in attempting a play, was to avoid every appearance of plagiary, I thought I should stand a better chance of effecting this from being in a walk which I had not frequented, and where consequently the progress of invention was less likely to be interrupted by starts of recollection: for on subjects on which the mind has been much informed, invention is slow of exerting itself. Faded ideas float in the fancy like half-forgotten dreams; and the imagination in its fullest enjoyments becomes suspicious of its offspring, and doubts whether it has created or adopted.

With regard to some particular passages which on the first

35 *candour* freedom from bias against something, so that it comes to mean also a willingness to think favourably

46 *exploded* rejected with scorn (*OED* sense 2)

63 *plagiary* plagiarism

---

50 *Mr Harris* the manager of Covent Garden, who did not usually concern himself with the details of productions

night's representation seemed generally disliked, I confess, that if I felt any emotion of surprise at the disapprobation, it was not that they were disapproved of, but that I had not before perceived that they deserved it. As some part of the attack on the piece was begun too early to pass for the sentence of judgement, which is ever tardy in condemning, it has been suggested to me, that much of the disapprobation must have arisen from virulence of malice, rather than severity of criticism: but as I was more apprehensive of there being just grounds to excite the latter, than conscious of having deserved the former, I continue not to believe that probable, which I am sure must have been unprovoked. However, if it was so, and I could even mark the quarter from whence it came, it would be ungenerous to retort; for no passion suffers more than malice from disappointment. For my own part, I see no reason why the author of a play should not regard a first night's audience, as a candid and judicious friend attending, in behalf of the public, at his last rehearsal. If he can dispense with flattery, he is sure at least of sincerity, and even though the annotation be rude, he may rely upon the justness of the comment. Considered in this light, that audience, whose *fiat* is essential to the poet's claim, whether his object be fame or profit, has surely a right to expect some deference to its opinion, from principles of politeness at least, if not from gratitude.

As for the little puny critics, who scatter their peevish strictures in private circles, and scribble at every author who has the eminence of being unconnected with them, as they are usually spleen-swollen from a vain idea of increasing their consequence, there will always be found a petulance and illiberality in their remarks, which should place them as far beneath the notice of a gentleman, as their original dullness had sunk them from the level of the most unsuccessful author.

It is not without pleasure that I catch at an opportunity of justifying myself from the charge of intending any national reflection in the character of Sir Lucius O'Trigger. If any gentlemen opposed the piece from that idea, I thank them sincerely for their opposition; and if the condemnation of this comedy (however misconceived the provocation) could have added one spark to the decaying flame of national attachment to the country supposed to

84 *mark* distinguish
92 *fiat* Latin, let it be done; hence, pronouncement
98 *spleen-swollen* full of spleen, i.e., ill-humoured, grudging, and spiteful

---

106 *the character of Sir Lucius* see Introduction, p. xiv

be reflected on, I should have been happy in its fate; and might with truth have boasted, that it had done more real service in its failure, than the successful morality of a thousand stage-novels will ever effect.

It is usual, I believe, to thank the performers in a new play, for the exertion of their several abilities. But where (as in this instance) their merit has been so striking and uncontroverted, as to call for the warmest and truest applause from a number of judicious audiences, the poet's after-praise comes like the feeble acclamation of a child to close the shouts of a multitude. The conduct, however, of the principals in a theatre cannot be so apparent to the public. I think it therefore but justice to declare, that from this theatre (the only one I can speak of from experience) those writers who wish to try the dramatic line, will meet with that candour and liberal attention, which are generally allowed to be better calculated to lead genius into excellence, than either the precepts of judgement, or the guidance of experience. THE AUTHOR

---

113 *stage-novels* probably referring to the sentimental comedies also condemned in the 'Prologue on the Tenth Night'; see Introduction, p. xvi–xviii

# PROLOGUE

BY THE AUTHOR
*Spoken by Mr Woodward and Mr Quick*

*Enter* SERJEANT AT LAW, *and* ATTORNEY *following, and giving a paper*

SERJEANT
What's here—a vile cramp hand! I cannot see
Without my spectacles.

ATTORNEY
He means his fee.
Nay, Mr Serjeant, good Sir, try again. *Gives money*

SERJEANT
The scrawl improves—(*More* [*money is given*]) O come, 'tis pretty plain.
Hey! how's this? Dibble! sure it cannot be!
A poet's brief! A poet and a fee!

ATTORNEY
Yea Sir!—though you without reward, I know,
Would gladly plead the muses' cause—

SERJEANT
So—So!

ATTORNEY
And if the fee offends—your wrath should fall
On me—

SERJEANT Dear Dibble no offence at all—

ATTORNEY
Some sons of Phoebus in the courts we meet,

SERJEANT
And fifty sons of Phoebus in the Fleet!

ATTORNEY
Nor pleads he worse, who with a decent sprig
Of bays adorns his legal waste of wig.

5 *Dibble* the attorney's name, perhaps from his bowing to the superior serjeant-at-law
11 *sons of Phoebus* poets (Phoebus Apollo the god of poetry)
12 *Fleet* the Fleet prison (where the poet might be imprisoned for debt)
14 *bays* laurel; i.e., writes poetry (from the laurel wreath of poets)

---

s.d. *Enter Serjeant-at-Law . . . paper* The Prologue, as is common, depends on a legal metaphor. The Serjeant-at-Law (or barrister) is given a brief, or summary of the case (the paper), by the attorney (or legal agent) to plead for the author before the court (the audience)

SERJEANT

Full-bottomed heroes thus, on signs, unfurl
A leaf of laurel—in a grove of curl!
Yet tell your client, that, in adverse days,
This wig is warmer than a bush of bays.

ATTORNEY

Do you then, Sir, my client's place supply,
Profuse of robe, and prodigal of tie—
Do you, with all those blushing powers of face,
And wonted bashful hesitating grace,
Rise in the court, and flourish on the case. *Exit*

SERJEANT

For practice then suppose—this brief will show it—
Me, Serjeant Woodward, counsel for the poet.
Used to the ground—I know 'tis hard to deal
With this dread court from whence there's no appeal;
No tricking here, to blunt the edge of law,
Or, damned in equity, escape by flaw:
But judgement given, your sentence must remain;
No writ of error lies to Drury Lane!
Yet when so kind you seem, 'tis past dispute
We gain some favour, if not costs of suit.
No spleen is here! I see no hoarded fury;
I think I never faced a milder jury!
Sad else our plight!—where frowns are transportation,
A hiss the gallows, and a groan, damnation!
But such the public candour, without fear
My client waives all right of challenge here.
No newsman from our session is dismissed,

20 *tie* i.e., tie wig (in which the false hair is gathered at the back)
23 *flourish* discourse elegantly
34 *spleen* ill-humour, prejudice
40 *newsman* journalist

---

15–16 *Full-bottomed . . . curl!* referring to their flowing wigs, with (ironically) a tiny laurel wreath (also used for conquerors) almost hidden in the huge wig
18 *This wig . . . bush of bays* the legal profession is more profitable than poetry
27–31 *With this dread court . . . Drury Lane!* In a court of law, a guilty person may escape on a technicality (1.29), or appeal to a higher court to set aside the judgment; but this is not possible in the theatre, since if Covent Garden condemns a play, there is no possibility that Drury Lane (the other main theatre) will praise it.
33 *costs of suit* in the theatrical sense, profit
39 *right of challenge* the right to dismiss potential jurors (here, the audience) as biased

Nor wit nor critic we scratch off the list;
His faults can never hurt another's ease,
His crime at worst—a bad attempt to please:
Thus, all respecting, he appeals to all,
And by the general voice will stand or fall.

# PROLOGUE

BY THE AUTHOR

*Spoken on the tenth night, by Mrs Bulkley*

Granted our cause, our suit and trial o'er,
The worthy Serjeant need appear no more:
In pleasing I a different client choose,
He served the poet—I would serve the muse:
Like him, I'll try to merit your applause,
A female counsel in a female's cause.
Look on this form—where humour quaint and sly,
Dimples the cheek, and points the beaming eye;
Where gay invention seems to boast its wiles
In amorous hint, and half-triumphant smiles;
While her light masks or covers satire's strokes,
All hide the conscious blush, her wit provokes.
Look on her well—does she seem formed to teach?
Should you expect to hear this lady—preach?
Is grey experience suited to her youth?
Do solemn sentiments become that mouth?
Bid her be grave, those lips should rebel prove
To every theme that slanders mirth or love.
Yet thus adorned with every graceful art
To charm the fancy and yet reach the heart
Must we displace her? And instead advance
The goddess of the woeful countenance—
The sentimental muse! Her emblems view
The *Pilgrim's Progress*, and a sprig of rue!
View her—too chaste to look like flesh and blood—
Primly portrayed on emblematic wood!
Thus fixed in usurpation should she stand
She'll snatch the dagger from her sister's hand:
And having made her votaries weep a flood

12 *hide* ed. (hides 1776)
24 *rue* the herb; punningly, sorrow, regret

---

7 *on this form* pointing to the figure of Comedy which stood on one side of the stage
23 *sentimental muse* pathetic comedies, which excited tears and pathos as much as laughter, and which depended on the idea of man's natural virtue
24 *Pilgrim's Progress* as an example of crude (and ungentlemanly) moral writing
28 *sister's* tragedy's (the sister of comedy)

Good heaven! she'll end her comedies in blood—
Bid Harry Woodward break poor Dunstall's crown!
Imprison Quick—and knock Ned Shuter down;
While sad Barsanti—weeping o'er the scene,
Shall stab herself—or poison Mrs Green.
Such dire encroachments to prevent in time,
Demands the critic's voice—the poet's rhyme.
Can our light scenes add strength to holy laws!
Such puny patronage but hurts the cause:
Fair virtue scorns our feeble aid to ask;
And moral truth disdains the trickster's mask.
For here their favourite stands, whose brow—severe
And sad—claims youth's respect, and pity's tear;
Who—when oppressed by foes her worth creates—
Can point a poignard at the guilt she hates.

---

31–4 *Woodward . . . Mrs Green* actors and actresses in the first performances of *The Rivals*

41 *their favourite* pointing to the figure of Tragedy on the other side of the stage

## DRAMATIS PERSONAE

### Men

| | |
|---|---|
| SIR ANTHONY ABSOLUTE | *Mr Shuter* |
| CAPTAIN ABSOLUTE | *Mr Woodward* |
| FAULKLAND | *Mr Lewis* |
| ACRES | *Mr Quick* |
| SIR LUCIUS O'TRIGGER | *Mr Clinch* |
| FAG | *Mr Lee Lewes* |
| DAVID | *Mr Dunstall* |
| COACHMAN | *Mr Fearon* |
| [ERRAND BOY | |
| SERVANTS] | |

### Women

| | |
|---|---|
| MRS MALAPROP | *Mrs Green* |
| LYDIA LANGUISH | *Miss Barsanti* |
| JULIA | *Mrs Bulkley* |
| LUCY | *Mrs Lessingham* |
| [MAID] | |

Scene, *Bath*
Time of action, *within one day*

3 *Lewis* ed. (Lewes 1775)
6 FAG a drudge (as in the English public-school usage)
6 *Lee Lewes* ed. (Lee-Lewis 1775)
7 *Dunstall* ed. (Dunstal 1775)
9 MALAPROP from the French *mal à propos,* inappropriate
s.d. *within one day* 1776 (Five Hours 1775)

---

1 *Absolute* Sir Anthony is 'absolute' in two ways; he is arbitrary and tyrannical as a father, and precise in his manner of speech

2 *Mr Woodward* Woodward was sixty when he created this role. See Cecil Price, *Theatre in the Age of Garrick* (Oxford, 1973), p. 37

4 *Acres* his name and the name of his home (Clod Hall) show the character as a country booby

5 *O'Trigger* referring to his love of duelling (a characteristic of the stage Irishman)
*Mr Clinch* later in 1775 Sheridan wrote a farce, *St Patrick's Day,* for Clinch's benefit performance, in gratitude for his successful performance of Sir Lucius

10 *Languish* Lydia might well 'languish' on a couch, as a sentimental attitude

# THE RIVALS

## Act I, Scene i

*[Scene,] a street in Bath*

COACHMAN *crosses the stage. Enter* FAG, *looking after him*

FAG

What!—Thomas!—Sure 'tis he?—What!—Thomas! —Thomas!

COACHMAN

Hey!—Odds life!—Mr Fag!—give us your hand, my old fellow-servant.

FAG

Excuse my glove, Thomas: I'm devilish glad to see you, my lad: why, my prince of charioteers, you look as hearty!—but who the deuce thought of seeing you in Bath!

COACHMAN

Sure, Master, Madam Julia, Harry, Mrs Kate, and the postillion be all come!

FAG

Indeed!

COACHMAN

Aye! Master thought another fit of the gout was coming to make him a visit: so he'd a mind to gi't the slip, and whip we were all off at an hour's warning.

FAG

Aye, aye! hasty in everything, or it would not be Sir Anthony Absolute!

COACHMAN

But tell us, Mr Fag, how does young Master? Odd! Sir Anthony will stare to see the Captain here!

FAG

I do not serve Captain Absolute now—

COACHMAN

Why sure!

FAG

At present I am employed by Ensign Beverley.

3 *Odds* a euphemism for 'God's'

11 *Aye* used either for 'yes' or, as here, for emphasis, 'certainly'

20 *Ensign* the lowest rank of commissioned officer in the infantry

COACHMAN

I doubt, Mr Fag, you ha'n't changed for the better.

FAG

I have not changed, Thomas.

COACHMAN

No! why didn't you say you had left young Master?

FAG

No—well, honest Thomas, I must puzzle you no farther: briefly then—Captain Absolute and Ensign Beverley are one and the same person.

COACHMAN

The devil they are!

FAG

So it is indeed, Thomas; and the *Ensign* half of my master being on guard at present—the *Captain* has nothing to do with me.

COACHMAN

So, so!—what, this is some freak, I warrant! Do, tell us, Mr Fag, the meaning o't—you know I ha' trusted you.

FAG

You'll be secret, Thomas.

COACHMAN

As a coach-horse.

FAG

Why then the cause of all this is—L, O, V, E,—love, Thomas, who (as you may get read to you) has been a masquerader ever since the days of Jupiter.

COACHMAN

Aye, aye; I guessed there was a lady in the case: but pray, why does your master pass only for Ensign?—now if he had shammed General indeed——

FAG

Ah! Thomas, there lies the mystery o'the matter. Harkee, Thomas, my master is in love with a lady of a very singular taste: a lady who likes him better as a half-pay Ensign than

42 *singular* unusual, odd

---

37 *Jupiter* who took on various disguises (as animals and as mortal men) to woo mortal women

43 *half-pay* an ensign in a 'marching regiment' would receive 3 shillings a day subsistence, with the balance of his full pay of 3*s*. 8*d*. (less some stoppages) paid at Midsummer and Christmas, so that his total pay was about £60 to £65 a year. A captain, as Absolute is, would receive 7*s*.6*d*. subsistence, with the balance of his full pay of 10*s*. a day, minus the same stoppages but plus some profits from the administration of his company, paid at the same times, so that his total pay was about £180 or £190 a year

if she knew he was son and heir to Sir Anthony Absolute, a baronet with three thousand a year!

COACHMAN

That is an odd taste indeed!—but has she got the stuff, Mr Fag; is she rich, hey?

FAG

Rich!—why, I believe she owns half the stocks! Zounds! Thomas, she could pay the national debt as easy as I could my washerwoman! She has a lap-dog that eats out of gold—she feeds her parrot with small pearls—and all her thread-papers are made of bank-notes!

COACHMAN

Bravo!—faith!—odd! I warrant she has a set of thousands at least: but does she draw kindly with the Captain?

FAG

As fond as pigeons.

COACHMAN

May one hear her name?

FAG

Miss Lydia Languish—but there is an old tough aunt in the way; though by the bye—she has never seen my master—for he got acquainted with Miss while on a visit in Gloucestershire.

COACHMAN

Well—I wish they were once harnessed together in matrimony. But pray, Mr Fag, what kind of a place is this Bath? I ha' heard a deal of it—here's a mort o' merry-making—hey?

FAG

Pretty well, Thomas, pretty well—'tis a good lounge. In

48 *stocks* here probably investments in the National Debt
51 *thread-papers* strips of paper folded in creases to hold skeins of thread
63 *mort* great deal (a dialect word)
65 *lounge* place for idling away the time

---

53 *set of thousands* various explanations have been suggested, the most likely of which seems 'a quantity of thousands', i.e., a great deal of money
54 *draw kindly* get on well; like 'secret as a coach horse' and 'harnessed together', the metaphor shows the speaker's preoccupation with his trade, since it refers to horses pulling together in harness

the morning we go to the pump-room (though neither my master nor I drink the waters); after breakfast we saunter on the parades or play a game at billiards; at night we dance: but damn the place, I'm tired of it: their regular hours stupefy me—not a fiddle nor a card after eleven!—however Mr Faulkland's gentleman and I keep it up a little in private parties; I'll introduce you there, Thomas—you'll like him much.

COACHMAN

Sure I know Mr Du-Peigne—you know his master is to marry Madam Julia.

FAG

I had forgot. But Thomas you must polish a little—indeed you must: here now—this wig!—what the devil do you do with a *wig,* Thomas? None of the London whips of any degree of ton wear wigs now.

COACHMAN

More's the pity! more's the pity, I say. Odds life! when I heard how the lawyers and doctors had took to their own hair, I thought how 'twould go next—odd rabbit it! when the fashion had got foot on the Bar, I guessed 'twould mount to the Box!—but 'tis all out of character, believe me, Mr Fag: and lookee, I'll never gi' up mine—the lawyers and doctors may do as they will.

78 *whips* coachmen
79 *ton* fashion, the smart set (a vogue word)
83 *Bar* the legal profession
84 *Box* the box on which the coachman sits; hence, coachmen

---

66 *pump-room* John Wood the elder, who rebuilt much of Bath in the first half of the eighteenth century, described the pump room as small, draughty, and inconvenient (*An Essay towards a description of Bath* (2nd ed., London, 1749), II, 269-70). It was, however, common for all visitors to assemble there in the morning, whether or not they drank the waters (see Wood, op. cit., II, 438; Tobias Smollett, *Humphrey Clinker*, ed. Angus Ross (Harmondsworth, 1967), pp. 68-9; Christopher Anstey, *The New Bath Guide* (9th ed., London, 1773, p. 71)

70 *after eleven* Beau Nash (1674-1761), who was principally responsible for Bath's development as a social centre in the earlier eighteenth century, had forbidden balls (which were held on Tuesdays and Fridays, and for which visitors paid a subscription) to continue after 11 o'clock, 'lest Invalids should be tempted to commit Irregularities' and so undo the benefit they gained from drinking the waters (see Wood, op. cit., II, 443)

74 *Du-Peigne* like so many of the characters, Faulkland's valet has a typifying name, 'of the comb'

FAG

Well, Thomas, we'll not quarrel about that.

COACHMAN

Why, bless you, the gentlemen of they professions ben't all of a mind—for in our village now tho'ff Jack Gauge the exciseman has ta'en to his carrots, there's little Dick the farrier swears he'll never forsake his bob, though all the college should appear with their own heads!

FAG

Indeed! well said Dick! but hold—mark! mark! Thomas.

COACHMAN

Zooks! 'tis the Captain—is that the lady with him?

FAG

No! no! that is Madam Lucy—my master's mistress's maid. They lodge at that house—but I must after him to tell him the news.

COACHMAN

Odd! he's giving her money!—well, Mr Fag——

FAG

Goodbye, Thomas—I have an appointment in Gyde's Porch this evening at eight; meet me there, and we'll make a little party. *Exeunt severally*

89 *tho'ff* dialect form of 'though'
90 *carrots* ginger hair
91 *farrier* blacksmith and horse doctor
91 *bob* a wig with the bottom in short curls
92 *college* of physicians or surgeons
94 *Zooks* a shortened form of 'gadzooks': a rustic oath

---

89 *Jack Gauge* a similar name; a gauger or exciseman calculated the capacity of casks of beer, wine, or spirits for duty to be levied on them
99 *Gyde's Porch* Gyde kept the lower assembly rooms

## [Act I,] Scene ii

*[Scene,] a dressing-room in* MRS MALAPROP*'s lodgings*
LYDIA *sitting on a sofa with a book in her hand.* LUCY, *as just returned from a message*

LUCY
Indeed, Ma'am, I transferred half the town in search of it: I don't believe there's a circulating library in Bath I ha'n't been at.

LYDIA
And could not you get *The Reward of Constancy*?

LUCY
No, indeed, Ma'am.

LYDIA
Nor *The Fatal Connection*?

LUCY
No, indeed, Ma'am.

LYDIA
Nor *The Mistakes of the Heart*?

LUCY
Ma'am, as ill-luck would have it, Mr Bull said Miss Sukey Saunter had just fetched it away.

LYDIA
Heigh-ho!— did you inquire for *The Delicate Distress*?

LUCY
Or *The Memoirs of Lady Woodford*? Yes indeed, Ma'am. I asked everywhere for it; and I might have brought it from Mr Frederick's, but Lady Slattern Lounger, who had just sent it home, had so soiled and dog's-eared it, it wa'n't fit for a Christian to read.

1 *transferred* 1775 (traversed 1776)

---

2 *circulating library* There were several in Bath at this time (see Wood, op. cit., II, 417-18; *Humphrey Clinker*, ed. cit., p. 70). It was conventional to attack them and the practice of novel-reading which they fostered (although many also had substantial stocks of serious works). See Paul Kaufman, 'The Community Library', *Transactions of the American Philosophical Society*, n.s. LVII, part 7 (Philadelpha, 1967), and 'In Defense of Fair Readers', *A Review of English Literature* VIII (1967), 68-77

4 *The Reward of Constancy* see Appendix for Lydia's books

9 *Mr Bull* Lewis Bull, who also sold books and knick-knacks. His shop was opposite Gyde's rooms on the Lower Walks

14 *Mr Frederick*, William Frederick, whose shop was at 18, The Grove. A catalogue of his library for 1774 is extant

LYDIA

Heigh-ho!—yes, I always know when Lady Slattern has been before me. She has a most observing thumb; and I believe cherishes her nails for the convenience of making marginal notes. Well, child, what *have* you brought me?

LUCY

Oh! here Ma'am. (*Taking books from under her cloak, and from her pockets*) This is *The Gordian Knot*—and this *Peregrine Pickle*. Here are *The Tears of Sensibility*, and *Humphrey Clinker*. This is *The Memoirs of a Lady of Quality, written by herself*—and here the second volume of *The Sentimental Journey*.

LYDIA

Heigh-ho!—what are those books by the glass?

LUCY

The great one is only *The Whole Duty of Man*—where I press a few blondes, Ma'am.

LYDIA

Very well—give me the *sal volatile*.

LUCY

Is it in a blue cover, Ma'am?

LYDIA

My smelling bottle, you simpleton!

LUCY

Oh, the drops!—here Ma'am.

LYDIA

Hold!—here's someone coming—quick, see who it is.

*Exit* LUCY

Surely I heard my cousin Julia's voice!

[*Enter*] LUCY

LUCY

Lud! Ma'am, here is Miss Melville.

LYDIA

Is it possible!

*Enter* JULIA [*Exit* LUCY]

LYDIA

My dearest Julia, how delighted am I! (*Embrace*) How unexpected was this happiness!

27 *glass* mirror

29 *blondes* pieces of lace originally made from unbleached silk

30 *sal volatile* an aromatic solution, used as a restorative by the 'delicate' in times of stress; smelling salts

JULIA

True, Lydia—and our pleasure is the greater; but what has been the matter? You were denied to me at first!

LYDIA

Ah! Julia, I have a thousand things to tell you! But first inform me, what has conjured you to Bath? Is Sir Anthony here?

JULIA

He is—we are arrived within this hour—and I suppose he will be here to wait on Mrs Malaprop as soon as he is dressed.

LYDIA

Then before we are interrupted, let me impart to you some of my distress! I know your gentle nature will sympathize with me, though your prudence may condemn me! My letters have informed you of my whole connection with Beverley—but I have lost him, Julia!—my aunt has discovered our intercourse by a note she intercepted, and has confined me ever since!—Yet, would you believe it? she has fallen absolutely in love with a tall Irish baronet she met one night since we have been here, at Lady Macshuffle's rout.

JULIA

You jest, Lydia!

LYDIA

No, upon my word. She really carries on a kind of correspondence with him, under a feigned name though, till she chooses to be known to him—but it is a *Delia* or a *Celia*, I assure you.

JULIA

Then, surely, she is now more indulgent to her niece.

LYDIA

Quite the contrary. Since she has discovered her own frailty, she is become more suspicious of mine. Then I must inform you of another plague! That odious Acres is to be in Bath today; so that I protest I shall be teased out of all spirits!

JULIA

Come, come, Lydia, hope the best—Sir Anthony shall use his interest with Mrs Malaprop.

47 *dressed* i.e., changed out of his dusty travelling clothes
57 *rout* party, social gathering

---

61 *Delia or a Celia* conventional names for a sweetheart or sought-for mistress in poetry

LYDIA

But you have not heard the worst. Unfortunately I had quarrelled with my poor Beverley, just before my aunt made the discovery, and I have not seen him since, to make it up.

JULIA

What was his offence?

LYDIA

Nothing at all! But, I don't know how it was, as often as we had been together, we had never had a quarrel! And, somehow I was afraid he would never give me an opportunity. So, last Thursday, I wrote a letter to myself, to inform myself that Beverley was at that time paying his addresses to another woman. I signed it *your Friend unknown*, showed it to Beverley, charged him with his falsehood, put myself in a violent passion, and vowed I'd never see him more.

JULIA

And you let him depart so, and have not seen him since?

LYDIA

'Twas the next day my aunt found the matter out. I intended only to have teased him three days and a half, and now I've lost him for ever.

JULIA

If he is as deserving and sincere as you have represented him to me, he will never give you up so. Yet consider, Lydia, you tell me he is but an ensign, and you have thirty thousand pounds!

LYDIA

But you know I lose most of my fortune, if I marry without my aunt's consent, till of age; and that is what I have determined to do, ever since I knew the penalty. Nor could I love the man, who would wish to wait a day for the alternative.

JULIA

Nay, this is caprice!

LYDIA

What, does Julia tax me with caprice? I thought her lover Faulkland had inured her to it.

JULIA

I do not love even *his* faults.

LYDIA

But apropos—you have sent to him, I suppose?

102 *apropos* with regard to (Faulkland)

JULIA

Not yet, upon my word—nor has he the least idea of my being in Bath. Sir Anthony's resolution was so sudden, I could not inform him of it.

LYDIA

Well, Julia, you are your own mistress (though under the protection of Sir Anthony), yet have you, for this long year, been a slave to the caprice, the whim, the jealousy of this ungrateful Faulkland, who will ever delay assuming the right of a husband, while you suffer him to be equally imperious as a lover.

JULIA

Nay you are wrong entirely. We were contracted before my father's death. *That*, and some consequent embarrassments, have delayed what I know to be my Faulkland's most ardent wish. He is too generous to trifle on such a point. And for his character, you wrong him there too—no, Lydia, he is too proud, too noble to be jealous; if he is captious, 'tis without dissembling; if fretful, without rudeness. Unused to the fopperies of love, he is negligent of the little duties expected from a lover—but being unhackneyed in the passion, his affection is ardent and sincere; and as it engrosses his whole soul, he expects every thought and emotion of his mistress to move in unison with his. Yet, though his pride calls for this full return—his humility makes him undervalue those qualities in him, which would entitle him to it; and not feeling why he should be loved to the degree he wishes, he still suspects that he is not loved enough. This temper, I must own, has cost me many unhappy hours; but I have learned to think myself his debtor, for those imperfections which arise from the ardour of his attachment.

LYDIA

Well, I cannot blame you for defending him. But tell me candidly, Julia, had he never saved your life, do you think you should have been attached to him as you are? Believe me, the rude blast that overset your boat was a prosperous gale of love to him.

JULIA

Gratitude may have strengthened my attachment to Mr

113 *embarrassments* impediments

118 *captious* too apt to find fault; hypersensitive

121 *unhackneyed* inexperienced, and therefore not regarding courtship as routine

Faulkland, but I loved him before he had preserved me; yet surely that alone were an obligation sufficient——

LYDIA

Obligation! Why a water-spaniel would have done as much! Well, I should never think of giving my heart to a man because he could swim!

JULIA

Come, Lydia, you are too inconsiderate.

LYDIA

Nay, I do but jest—what's here?

*Enter* LUCY *in a hurry*

LUCY

O Ma'am, here is Sir Anthony Absolute just come home with your aunt.

LYDIA

They'll not come here—Lucy, do you watch. *Exit* LUCY

JULIA

Yet I must go—Sir Anthony does not know I am here, and if we meet, he'll detain me, to show me the town. I'll take another opportunity of paying my respects to Mrs Malaprop, when she shall treat me, as long as she chooses, with her select words so ingeniously *misapplied,* without being *mispronounced.*

[*Enter*] LUCY

LUCY

O Lud! Ma'am, they are both coming upstairs.

LYDIA

Well, I'll not detain you coz—adieu, my dear Julia, I'm sure you are in haste to send to Faulkland. There—through my room you'll find another staircase.

JULIA

Adieu. (*Embrace*) *Exit* JULIA

LYDIA

Here, my dear Lucy, hide these books—quick, quick—fling *Peregrine Pickle* under the toilet—throw *Roderick Random* into the closet—put *The Innocent Adultery* into

155 *coz* cousin
160 *toilet* dressing-table
161 *closet* cupboard

---

160 *Peregrine Pickle* see Appendix

*The Whole Duty of Man*—thrust *Lord Aimworth* under the sofa—cram Ovid behind the bolster—there—put *The Man of Feeling* into your pocket—so, so, now lay Mrs Chapone in sight, and leave Fordyce's *Sermons* open on the table.

LUCY

O burn it, Ma'am, the hairdresser has torn away as far as 'Proper Pride'.

LYDIA

Never mind—open at 'Sobriety'—fling me Lord Chesterfield's *Letters*. Now for 'em. [*Exit* LUCY]

*Enter* MRS MALAPROP *and* SIR ANTHONY ABSOLUTE

MRS MALAPROP

There, Sir Anthony, there sits the deliberate simpleton, who wants to disgrace her family, and lavish herself on a fellow not worth a shilling!

LYDIA

Madam, I thought you once——

MRS MALAPROP

You thought, Miss! I don't know any business you have to think at all—thought does not become a young woman; the point we would request of you is, that you will promise to forget this fellow—to illiterate him, I say, quite from your memory.

LYDIA

Ah! Madam! our memories are independent of our wills. It is not so easy to forget.

MRS MALAPROP

But I say it is, Miss; there is nothing on earth so easy as to *forget*, if a person chooses to set about it. I'm sure I have as much forgot your poor dear uncle as if he had never existed—and I thought it my duty so to do; and let me tell you, Lydia, these violent memories don't become a young woman.

SIR ANTHONY

Why sure she won't pretend to remember what she's ordered not! Aye, this comes of her reading!

163 *bolster* a long pillow or cushion
176 *woman; the* 1775 (woman. But the 1776)
178 *illiterate* for, obliterate
184 *forgot* i.e., forgotten (a possible eighteenth-century usage)

---

167 *torn away* i.e., to make curl papers, used instead of hair-rollers

LYDIA

What crime, Madam, have I committed to be treated thus?

MRS MALAPROP

Now don't attempt to extirpate yourself from the matter; you know I have proof controvertible of it. But tell me, will you promise to do as you're bid? Will you take a husband of your friend's choosing?

LYDIA

Madam, I must tell you plainly, that had I no preference for anyone else, the choice you have made would be my aversion.

MRS MALAPROP

What business have you, Miss, with *preference* and *aversion*? They don't become a young woman; and you ought to know, that as both always wear off, 'tis safest in matrimony to begin with a little aversion. I am sure I hated your poor dear uncle before marriage as if he'd been a blackamoor—and yet, Miss, you are sensible what a wife I made!—and when it pleased Heaven to release me from him, 'tis unknown what tears I shed! But suppose we were going to give you another choice, will you promise us to give up this Beverley?

LYDIA

Could I belie my thoughts so far, as to give that promise, my actions would certainly as far belie my words.

MRS MALAPROP

Take yourself to your room. You are fit company for nothing but your own ill-humours.

LYDIA

Willingly, Ma'am—I cannot change for the worse.

*Exit* LYDIA

MRS MALAPROP

There's a little intricate hussy for you!

SIR ANTHONY

It is not to be wondered at, Ma'am—all this is the natural consequence of teaching girls to read. Had I a thousand daughters, by heaven! I'd as soon have them taught the black art as their alphabet!

191 *extirpate* root out or exterminate: for, extricate or exculpate
192 *controvertible* for, incontrovertible
194 *friend's* relation's
203 *sensible* aware
213 *intricate* perplexed or complicated: for, ingrate?

MRS MALAPROP

Nay, nay, Sir Anthony, you are an absolute misanthropy!

SIR ANTHONY

In my way hither, Mrs Malaprop, I observed your niece's maid coming forth from a circulating library! She had a book in each hand—they were half-bound volumes, with marble covers! From that moment I guessed how full of duty I should see her mistress!

MRS MALAPROP

Those are vile places, indeed!

SIR ANTHONY

Madam, a circulating library in a town is as an ever-green tree of diabolical knowledge! It blossoms through the year! And depend on it, Mrs Malaprop, that they who are so fond of handling the leaves, will long for the fruit at last.

MRS MALAPROP

Well, but Sir Anthony, your wife, Lady Absolute, was fond of books.

SIR ANTHONY

Aye—and injury sufficient they were to her, Madam. But were I to choose another helpmate, the extent of her erudition should consist in her knowing her simple letters, without their mischievous combinations; and the summit of her science be—her ability to count as far as twenty. The first, Mrs Malaprop, would enable her to work A.A. upon my linen; and the latter would be quite sufficient to prevent her giving me a shirt, No.1 and a stock, No.2.

MRS MALAPROP

Fie, fie, Sir Anthony, you surely speak laconically!

SIR ANTHONY

Why, Mrs Malaprop, in moderation, now, what would you have a woman know?

MRS MALAPROP

Observe me, Sir Anthony. I would by no means wish a

218 *misanthropy* for, misanthrope, or misogynist?
229-38 *Well, but Sir Anthony . . . stock, No. 2.* 1775 (omitted 1776)
235 *science* knowledge
238 *stock* a close-fitting neckcloth
239 *laconically* using as few words as possible: for, ironically
242 *Observe* pay attention to

221-2 *half-bound . . . covers* with the spine and corners bound in leather, and the rest covered in marbled paper; i.e., novels
225 *ever-green* a compressed allusion to Genesis ii, 17 and Psalm xxxvii, 35
238 *stock, No. 2* Sir Anthony's precision extends to having his linen numbered in sets

daughter of mine to be a progeny of learning; I don't think so much learning becomes a young woman; for instance—I would never let her meddle with Greek, or Hebrew, or Algebra, or Simony, or Fluxions, or Paradoxes, or such inflammatory branches of learning —neither would it be necessary for her to handle any of your mathematical, astronomical, diabolical instruments. But, Sir Anthony, I would send her, at nine years old, to a boarding-school, in order to learn a little ingenuity and artifice. Then, Sir, she should have a supercilious knowledge in accounts; and as she grew up, I would have her instructed in geometry, that she might know something of the contagious countries; but above all, Sir Anthony, she should be mistress of orthodoxy, that she might not misspell, and mispronounce words so shamefully as girls usually do; and likewise that she might reprehend the true meaning of what she is saying. This, Sir Anthony, is what I would have a woman know; and I don't think there is a superstitious article in it.

SIR ANTHONY

Well, well, Mrs Malaprop, I will dispute the point no further with you; though I must confess, that you are a truly moderate and polite arguer, for almost every third word you say is on my side of the question. But, Mrs Malaprop, to the more important point in debate—you say, you have no objection to my proposal.

MRS MALAPROP

None, I assure you. I am under no positive engagement

243 *progeny* offspring, descendant: for, prodigy
246 *Simony* the crime of buying or selling church offices: for cyclometry? or ciphering?
246 *Fluxions* calculus (in Newtonian geometry)
246 *Paradoxes* for, parallaxes? (a term used in astronomy, a science popular among lay people in the earlier eighteenth century)
252 *artifice* two meanings are possible: trick or fraud; or, a skill obtained by practice
252 *supercilious* for, superficial
254 *geometry* for, geography
255 *contagious* for, contiguous
256 *orthodoxy* for, orthography
258 *reprehend* for, comprehend
261 *superstitious* for, superfluous: or possibly in the obsolete sense of over-scrupulous

---

268-9 . . . *engagement with Mr Acres* not a malapropism for Mrs Malaprop's being betrothed to Acres instead of Lydia; she has entered into no formal agreement with him for the disposal of Lydia with Mr Acres, and as Lydia is so obstinate against him, perhaps your son may have better success.

SIR ANTHONY

Well, Madam, I will write for the boy directly. He knows not a syllable of this yet, though I have for some time had the proposal in my head. He is at present with his regiment.

MRS MALAPROP

We have never seen your son, Sir Anthony; but I hope no objection on his side.

SIR ANTHONY

Objection!—let him object if he dare! No, no, Mrs Malaprop, Jack knows that the least demur puts me in a frenzy directly. My process was always very simple—in their younger days, 'twas 'Jack, do this'—if he demurred—I knocked him down—and if he grumbled at that—I always sent him out of the room.

MRS MALAPROP

Aye, and the properest way, o' my conscience!—nothing is so conciliating to young people as severity. Well, Sir Anthony, I shall give Mr Acres his discharge, and prepare Lydia to receive your son's invocations; and I hope you will represent her to the Captain as an object not altogether illegible.

SIR ANTHONY

Madam, I will handle the subject prudently. Well, I must leave you—and let me beg you, Mrs Malaprop, to enforce this matter roundly to the girl; take my advice—keep a tight hand—if she rejects the proposal—clap her under lock and key: and if you were just to let the servants forget to bring her dinner for three or four days, you can't conceive how she'd come about! *Exit* SIR ANTHONY

MRS MALAPROP

Well, at any rate I shall be glad to get her from under my intuition. She has somehow discovered my partiality for Sir Lucius O'Trigger—sure, Lucy can't have betrayed me! No, the girl is such a simpleton, I should have made her confess it. Lucy!—Lucy! (*Calls*) Had she been one of

284 *conciliating* pleasing: the sense requires the opposite
286 *invocations* possibly not a malapropism: or for, addresses
288 *illegible* for, ineligible
297 *intuition* for, tuition

your artificial ones, I should never have trusted her.

*Enter* LUCY

LUCY
Did you call, Ma'am?

MRS MALAPROP
Yes, girl. Did you see Sir Lucius while you was out?

LUCY
No, indeed, Ma'am, not a glimpse of him.

MRS MALAPROP
You are sure, Lucy, that you never mentioned——

LUCY
O gemini! I'd sooner cut my tongue out.

MRS MALAPROP
Well, don't let your simplicity be imposed on.

LUCY
No, Ma'am.

MRS MALAPROP
So, come to me presently, and I'll give you another letter to Sir Lucius; but mind Lucy—if ever you betray what you are entrusted with (unless it be other people's secrets to me) you forfeit my malevolence for ever: and your being a simpleton shall be no excuse for your locality.

*Exit* MRS MALAPROP

LUCY
Ha! ha! ha! So, my dear *simplicity*, let me give you a little respite—(*Altering her manner*) let girls in my station be as fond as they please of appearing expert, and knowing in their trusts; commend me to a mask of silliness, and a pair of sharp eyes for my own interest under it! Let me see to what account I have turned my *simplicity* lately—(*Looks at a paper*) *For abetting Miss Lydia Languish in a design of running away with an ensign—in money—sundry times—twelve pound twelve—gowns, five—hats, ruffles, caps, etc, etc.—numberless! From the said Ensign, within this last month, six guineas and a half*—about a quarter's pay! Item, *from Mrs Malaprop, for betraying the young people to her*—when I found matters were likely to be discovered—*two*

301 *artificial* possibly not a malapropism, in the obsolete sense of affected in manners: or for, artful

303 *was* a possible eighteenth-century usage

306 *gemini* a mild, and vulgar, oath

312 *malevolence* for, benevolence

313 *locality* for, loquacity

*guineas, and a black paduasoy.* Item, *from Mr Acres, for carrying divers letters*—which I never delivered—*two guineas, and a pair of buckles.* Item, *from Sir Lucius O'Trigger—three crowns—two gold pocket-pieces—and a silver snuff-box*!—Well done, *simplicity*!—yet I was forced to make my Hibernian believe, that he was corresponding, not with the aunt, but with the niece: for, though not over rich, I found he had too much pride and delicacy to sacrifice the feelings of a gentleman to the necessities of his fortune. *Exit*

## Act II, Scene i

[*Scene,*] CAPTAIN ABSOLUTE'*s lodgings*
CAPTAIN ABSOLUTE *and* FAG

FAG
Sir, while I was there, Sir Anthony came in: I told him, you had sent me to inquire after his health, and to know if he was at leisure to see you.

ABSOLUTE
And what did he say, on hearing I was at Bath?

FAG
Sir, in my life I never saw an elderly gentleman more astonished! He started back two or three paces, rapped out a dozen interjectural oaths, and asked, what the devil had brought you here!

ABSOLUTE
Well, Sir, and what did you say?

FAG
Oh, I lied, Sir—I forget the precise lie, but you may depend on't; he got no truth from me. Yet, with submission, for fear of blunders in future, I should be glad to fix what *has* brought us to Bath: in order that we may lie a little consistently. Sir Anthony's servants were curious, Sir, very curious indeed.

327 *paduasoy* heavy corded silk; a gown of that material
328 *divers* various
330 *crowns* five-shilling pieces
330 *pocket-pieces* coins no longer current, or similar small objects, carried as lucky charms
332 *Hibernian* Irishman
7 *interjectural* thrown in parenthetically

ABSOLUTE

You have said nothing to them——

FAG

Oh, not a word, Sir—not a word. Mr Thomas, indeed, the coachman (whom I take to be the discreetest of whips)——

ABSOLUTE

'Sdeath!—you rascal! you have not trusted him!

FAG

Oh, *no,* Sir—no—no—not a syllable, upon my veracity! He was, indeed, a little inquisitive; but I was sly, Sir—devilish sly! My master (said I) honest Thomas (you know, Sir, one says *honest* to one's inferiors) is come to Bath to *recruit*—yes, Sir—I said, *to recruit*—and whether for men, money, or constitution, you know, Sir, is nothing to him, nor anyone else.

ABSOLUTE

Well—recruit will do—let it be so——

FAG

Oh, Sir, recruit will do surprisingly—indeed, to give the thing an air, I told Thomas, that your honour had already enlisted five disbanded chairmen, seven minority waiters, and thirteen billiard markers.

ABSOLUTE

You blockhead, never say more than is necessary.

FAG

I beg pardon, Sir—I beg pardon. But with submission, a lie is nothing unless one supports it. Sir, whenever I draw on my invention for a good current lie, I always forge *endorsements*, as well as the bill.

22 *honest* used, as Fag points out, as a patronizing term of vague praise

---

24 *recruit* in three senses, amplified respectively by 'men', 'money', and 'constitution' (or health, vitality); enlist for the army: get a fresh supply of (i.e., by marrying an heiress like Lydia; Bath was a marriage market): restore

30 *disbanded chairmen* dismissed or unemployed men who had formerly carried sedan chairs or wheeled Bath chairs. Wood mentions complaints about the insolence and belligerence of the chairmen (op. cit., II, 412)

30 *minority waiters* various suggestions have been made; youthful waiters: waiters out of work or not regularly employed: waiters in a minority in some contemporary dispute

ABSOLUTE

Well, take care you don't hurt your credit, by offering too much security. Is Mr Faulkland returned?

FAG

He is above, Sir, changing his dress.

ABSOLUTE

Can you tell whether he has been informed of Sir Anthony's and Miss Melville's arrival?

FAG

I fancy not, Sir; he has seen no one since he came in, but his gentleman, who was with him at Bristol. I think, Sir, I hear Mr Faulkland coming down——

ABSOLUTE

Go, tell him I am here.

FAG

Yes, Sir—(*Going*) I beg pardon, Sir, but should Sir Anthony call, you will do me the favour to remember, that we are *recruiting*, if you please.

ABSOLUTE

Well, well.

FAG

And in tenderness to my character, if your honour could bring in the chairmen and waiters, I shall esteem it as an obligation; for though I never scruple a lie to serve my master, yet it hurts one's conscience, to be found out. *Exit*

ABSOLUTE

Now for my whimsical friend—if he does not know that his mistress is here, I'll tease him a little before I tell him——

*Enter* FAULKLAND

Faulkland, you're welcome to Bath again; you are punctual in your return.

FAULKLAND

Yes; I had nothing to detain me, when I had finished the business I went on. Well, what news since I left you? How stand matters between you and Lydia?

52 *scruple a lie* hesitate to lie when it is expedient

38 *security* Absolute takes up Fag's financial metaphor: Fag's invention or imagination is the (specious) credit on which he draws for an explanation that will appear plausible, as a false cheque, or bill, may pass for good money; Fag amplifies his lie to make it appear more plausible, as a forger might add confirming signatures to a false cheque. Absolute warns him not to make the lie look too good to be true

ABSOLUTE

Faith, much as they were; I have not seen her since our quarrel, however I expect to be recalled every hour.

FAULKLAND

Why don't you persuade her to go off with you at once?

ABSOLUTE

What, and lose two thirds of her fortune? You forget that my friend. No, no, I could have brought her to that long ago.

FAULKLAND

Nay then, you trifle too long—if you are sure of *her*, write to the aunt in your own character, and write to Sir Anthony for his consent.

ABSOLUTE

Softly, softly, for though I am convinced my little Lydia would elope with me as Ensign Beverley, yet am I by no means certain that she would take me with the impediments of our friends' consent, a regular humdrum wedding, and the reversion of a good fortune on my side; no, no, I must prepare her gradually for the discovery, and make myself necessary to her, before I risk it. Well, but Faulkland, you'll dine with us today at the hotel?

FAULKLAND

Indeed I cannot: I am not in spirits to be of such a party.

ABSOLUTE

By heavens! I shall forswear your company. You are the most teasing, captious, incorrigible lover! Do love like a man.

FAULKLAND

I own I am unfit for company.

ABSOLUTE

Am not *I* a lover; aye, and a romantic one too? Yet do I carry everywhere with me such a confounded farrago of doubts, fears, hopes, wishes, and all the flimsy furniture of a country miss's brain!

FAULKLAND

Ah! Jack, your heart and soul are not, like mine, fixed immutably on one only object. You throw for a large stake, but losing—you could stake, and throw again: but I have set my sum of happiness on this cast, and not to succeed, were to be stripped of all.

74 *reversion* certain of inheriting

84 *farrago* hotchpotch

90 *cast* throw of the dice

ABSOLUTE

But for heaven's sake! What grounds for apprehension can your whimsical brain conjure up at present?

FAULKLAND

What grounds for apprehension did you say? Heavens! are there not a thousand! I fear for her spirits—her health—her life. My absence may fret her; her anxiety for my return, her fears for me, may oppress her gentle temper. And for her health—does not every hour bring me cause to be alarmed? If it rains, some shower may even then have chilled her delicate frame! If the wind be keen, some rude blast may have affected her! The heat of noon, the dews of the evening, may endanger the life of her, for whom only I value mine. O Jack, when delicate and feeling souls are separated, there is not a feature in the sky, not a movement of the elements, not an aspiration of the breeze, but hints some cause for a lover's apprehension!

ABSOLUTE

Aye, but we may choose whether we will take the hint or not. So then, Faulkland, if you were convinced that Julia were well and in spirits, you would be entirely content?

FAULKLAND

I should be happy beyond measure—I am anxious only for that.

ABSOLUTE

Then to cure your anxiety at once—Miss Melville is in perfect health, and is at this moment in Bath.

FAULKLAND

Nay Jack—don't trifle with me.

ABSOLUTE

She is arrived here with my father within this hour.

FAULKLAND

Can you be serious?

ABSOLUTE

I thought you knew Sir Anthony better than to be surprised at a sudden whim of this kind. Seriously then, it is as I tell you—upon my honour.

FAULKLAND

My dear friend! Hollo, Du-Peigne! my hat—my dear Jack—now nothing on earth can give me a moment's uneasiness.

105 *aspiration* movement

*Enter* FAG

FAG

Sir, Mr Acres just arrived is below.

ABSOLUTE

Stay, Faulkland, this Acres lives within a mile of Sir Anthony, and he shall tell you how your mistress has been ever since you left her. Fag, show the gentleman up.

*Exit* FAG

FAULKLAND

What, is he much acquainted in the family?

ABSOLUTE

Oh, very intimate: I insist on your not going: besides, his character will divert you.

FAULKLAND

Well, I should like to ask him a few questions.

ABSOLUTE

He is likewise a rival of mine—that is of my other self's, for he does not think his friend Captain Absolute ever saw the lady in question—and it is ridiculous enough to hear him complain to me of one Beverley, a concealed skulking rival, who——

FAULKLAND

Hush! He's here.

*Enter* ACRES

ACRES

Hah! my dear friend, noble captain, and honest Jack, how do'st thou? Just arrived faith, as you see. [*To* FAULKLAND] Sir, your humble servant.—Warm work on the roads Jack—odds whips and wheels, I've travelled like a comet, with a tail of dust all the way as long as the Mall.

ABSOLUTE

Ah! Bob, you are indeed an eccentric planet, but we know your attraction hither—give me leave to introduce Mr Faulkland to you; Mr Faulkland, Mr Acres.

141 *Mall* a walk bordered by trees alongside St James's Park

---

136 s.d. *Enter* ACRES throughout this scene Absolute is the medium between Faulkland and Acres, who are both involved in their own little worlds, and communicate with each other via Absolute

140 *odds whips and wheels* the first example of Acre's 'referential' oaths (see 306), which are metonymic in form; thus here, whips and wheels are used as connected with travelling

142 *eccentric* Absolute puns on the astronomical and the colloquial senses

ACRES

Sir, I am most heartily glad to see you: Sir, I solicit your connections. Hey Jack—what this is Mr Faulkland, who——

ABSOLUTE

Aye, Bob, Miss Melville's Mr Faulkland.

ACRES

Odso! she and your father can be but just arrived before me—I suppose you have seen them. Ah! Mr Faulkland, you are indeed a happy man.

FAULKLAND

I have not seen Miss Melville yet, Sir—I hope she enjoyed full health and spirits in Devonshire?

ACRES

Never knew her better in my life, Sir—never better. Odds blushes and blooms! she has been as healthy as the German Spa.

FAULKLAND

Indeed!—I did hear that she had been a little indisposed.

ACRES

False, false, Sir—only said to vex you: quite the reverse, I assure you.

FAULKLAND

There, Jack, you see she has the advantage of me; I had almost fretted myself ill.

ABSOLUTE

Now you are angry with your mistress for not having been sick.

FAULKLAND

No, no, you misunderstand me: yet surely a little trifling indisposition is not an unnatural consequence of absence from those we love. Now confess—isn't there something unkind in this violent, robust, unfeeling health?

ABSOLUTE

Oh, it was very unkind of her to be well in your absence to be sure!

ACRES

Good apartments, Jack.

145-6 *solicit your connections* i.e., look forward to knowing you better
149 *Odso* a form of 'Godso', a mild oath

---

156 *German Spa* the name of a place (now in Belgium), now used generically for a town built round a mineral spring

FAULKLAND

Well Sir, but you were saying that Miss Melville has been so *exceedingly* well—what then she has been merry and gay I suppose? Always in spirits—hey?

ACRES

Merry, odds crickets! she has been the belle and spirit of the company wherever she has been—so lively and entertaining! so full of wit and humour!

FAULKLAND

There, Jack, there. Oh, by my soul! there is an innate levity in woman, that nothing can overcome. What! happy, and I away!

ABSOLUTE

Have done: how foolish this is! Just now you were only apprehensive for your mistress's spirits.

FAULKLAND

Why Jack, have I been the joy and spirit of the company?

ABSOLUTE

No indeed, you have not.

FAULKLAND

Have I been lively and entertaining?

ABSOLUTE

Oh, upon my word, I acquit you.

FAULKLAND

Have I been full of wit and humour?

ABSOLUTE

No, faith, to do you justice, you have been confoundedly stupid indeed.

ACRES

What's the matter with this gentleman?

ABSOLUTE

He is only expressing his great satisfaction at hearing that Julia has been so well and happy—that's all—hey, Faulkland?

FAULKLAND

Oh! I am rejoiced to hear it—yes, yes, she has a *happy* disposition!

ACRES

That she has indeed—then she is so accomplished—so sweet a voice—so expert at her harpsichord—such a mistress of flat and sharp, squallante, rumblante, and

---

197-8 *squallante, rumblante, and quiverante.* Acres makes quasi-Italian musical terms of squalling (hardly complimentary to Julia), rumbling, and quivering (perhaps *vibrato)*

quiverante! There was this time month—odds minims and crotchets! how she did chirrup at Mrs Piano's concert.

FAULKLAND

There again, what say you to this? You see she has been all mirth and song—not a thought of me!

ABSOLUTE

Pho! man, is not music the food of love?

FAULKLAND

Well, well, it may be so. Pray Mr—[*Aside to* ABSOLUTE] —what's his damned name?—Do you remember what songs Miss Melville sung?

ACRES

Not I, indeed.

ABSOLUTE

Stay now, they were some pretty, melancholy, purling stream airs, I warrant; perhaps you may recollect: did she sing 'When absent from my soul's delight'?

ACRES

No, that wa'n't it.

ABSOLUTE

Or 'Go, gentle gales!'—(*Sings*) 'Go, gentle gales!'

ACRES

O no! nothing like it. Odds! now I recollect one of them—(*Sings*) 'My heart's my own, my will is free'.

FAULKLAND

Fool! fool that I am! to fix all my happiness on such a trifler! 'Sdeath! to make herself the pipe and ballad-monger of a circle! to soothe her light heart with catches and glees! What can you say to this, Sir?

ABSOLUTE

Why, that I should be glad to hear my mistress had been so merry, Sir.

FAULKLAND

Nay, nay, nay—I am not sorry that she has been happy—no, no, I am glad of that—I would not have had her sad or sick—yet surely a sympathetic heart would have

198-9 *minims and crotchets* musical notes, by their time value
216 *catches* part songs or rounds and hence, ludicrous songs
217 *glees* unaccompanied part songs

---

199 *Piano* the Italian musical term for soft, gentle. The instrument, recently invented, was still known as a pianoforte
202 *music the food of love* cf. *Twelfth Night,* I. i, 1
207-8 *purling stream* a cliché of pastoral and love poetry
209 *When absent from my soul's delight* for the three songs mentioned, see Appendix

shown itself even in the choice of a song—she might have been temperately healthy, and somehow, plaintively gay; but she has been dancing too, I doubt not!

ACRES

What does the gentleman say about dancing?

ABSOLUTE

He says the lady we speak of dances as well as she sings.

ACRES

Aye truly, does she—there was at our last race-ball——

FAULKLAND

Hell and the devil! There! there!—I told you so! I told you so! Oh! she thrives in my absence!—dancing!—but her whole feelings have been in opposition with mine. I have been anxious, silent, pensive, sedentary—my days have been hours of care, my nights of watchfulness. She has been all health! spirit! laugh! song! dance!—Oh! damned, damned levity!

ABSOLUTE

For heaven's sake! Faulkland, don't expose yourself so. Suppose she has danced, what then?—does not the ceremony of society often oblige——

FAULKLAND

Well, well, I'll contain myself—perhaps, as you say—for form sake. What, Mr Acres, you were praising Miss Melville's manner of dancing a minuet—hey?

ACRES

Oh, I dare insure her for that—but what I was going to speak of was her country dancing: odds swimmings! she has such an air with her!

FAULKLAND

Now disappointment on her! Defend this, Absolute, why don't you defend this? Country dances! jigs, and reels! am I to blame now? A minuet I could have forgiven—I should not have minded that—I say I should not have regarded a minuet—but *country dances*! Zounds! had she made one in a cotillon—I believe I could have forgiven even that—but

241 *minuet* slow, stately dance first popular in the late seventeenth century

243 *swimmings* either giddiness (induced by the briskness of the country dance), or a smooth flowing motion

250 *cotillon* French dance introduced in the eighteenth century

---

243 *country dancing* in which couples stood face to face in long lines and in the movements of which partners mingled (hence Faulkland's objections). They were more lively than minuets

to be monkey-led for a night!—to run the gauntlet through a string of amorous palming puppies!—to show paces like a managed filly! O Jack, there never can be but *one* man in the world, whom a truly modest and delicate woman ought to pair with in a country dance; and even then, the rest of the couples should be her great uncles and aunts!

ABSOLUTE

Aye, to be sure!—grandfathers and grandmothers!

FAULKLAND

If there be but one vicious mind in the set, 'twill spread like a contagion—the action of their pulse beats to the lascivious movement of the jig—their quivering, warm-breathed sighs impregnate the very air—the atmosphere becomes electrical to love, and each amorous spark darts through every link of the chain! I must leave you—I own I am somewhat flurried—and that confounded looby has perceived it. *Going*

ABSOLUTE

Nay, but stay Faulkland, and thank Mr Acres for his good news.

FAULKLAND

Damn his news! *Exit* FAULKLAND

ABSOLUTE

Ha! ha! ha! poor Faulkland five minutes since—'nothing on earth could give him a moment's uneasiness'!

ACRES

The gentleman wa'n't angry at my praising his mistress, was he?

ABSOLUTE

A little jealous, I believe, Bob.

ACRES

You don't say so? Ha! ha! jealous of me—that's a good joke.

ABSOLUTE

There's nothing strange in that, Bob: let me tell you, that

251 *monkey-led* led (in the dances) by 'monkeys', i.e., fops

253 *managed* of a horse, put through the *manège* exercises; hence, exhibiting herself

263 *chain* line of dancers

264 *looby* awkward rustic

---

252 *palming* stroking with the palm; cf. *The Winter's Tale,* I. ii, 115 and 125-6, and *Othello* II. i, 166, in which there are heavy sexual innuendoes

262 *electrical* i.e., the atmosphere draws loving feelings out of the dancers

sprightly grace and insinuating manner of yours will do some mischief among the girls here.

ACRES

Ah! you joke—ha! ha! mischief—ha! ha! but you know I am not my own property, my dear Lydia has forestalled me. She could never abide me in the country, because I used to dress so badly—but odds frogs and tambours! I shan't take matters so here—now ancient Madam has no voice in it—I'll make my old clothes know who's master—I shall straightway cashier the hunting-frock—and render my leather breeches incapable. My hair has been in training some time.

ABSOLUTE

Indeed!

ACRES

Aye—and tho'ff the side-curls are a little restive, my hind-part takes to it very kindly.

ABSOLUTE

Oh, you'll polish, I doubt not.

ACRES

Absolutely I propose so—then if I can find out this Ensign Beverley, odds triggers and flints! I'll make him know the difference o't.

ABSOLUTE

Spoke like a man—but pray, Bob, I observe you have got an odd kind of a new method of swearing——

ACRES

Ha! ha! you've taken notice of it—'tis genteel, isn't it? I didn't invent it myself though; but a commander in our militia—a great scholar, I assure you—says that there is no meaning in the common oaths, and that nothing but their antiquity makes them respectable; because, he says, the

282 *frogs* ornamental fastenings consisting of a loop and a spindle-shaped button

282 *tambours* embroidery frames

283 *ancient Madam* i.e., his mother, 'the old lady'

285 *cashier* dismiss (in army use, dishonourably)

299 *militia* part-time soldiers raised in each county

---

293 *triggers and flints* of firearms; the flint made the spark which ignited the gunpowder and expelled the bullet

297 *genteel* now always used ironically (as it is by Absolute in 308), but in eighteenth-century usage, of persons, well bred, polite, elegant; of things, fashionable, elegant

ancients would never stick to an oath or two, but would say by Jove! or by Bacchus! or by Mars! or by Venus! or by Pallas! according to the sentiment—so that to swear with propriety, says my little major, the 'oath should be an echo to the sense'; and this we call the *oath referential,* or *sentimental swearing*—ha! ha! ha! 'tis genteel, isn't it?

ABSOLUTE
Very genteel, and very new indeed—and I dare say will supplant all other figures of imprecation.

ACRES
Aye, aye, the best terms will grow obsolete—damns have had their day.

*Enter* FAG

FAG
Sir, there is a gentleman below, desires to see you—shall I show him into the parlour?

ABSOLUTE
Aye—you may.

ACRES
Well, I must be gone——

ABSOLUTE
Stay; who is it, Fag?

FAG
Your father, Sir.

ABSOLUTE
You puppy, why didn't you show him up directly?
*Exit* FAG

ACRES
You have business with Sir Anthony—I expect a message from Mrs Malaprop at my lodgings—I have sent also to my dear friend Sir Lucius O'Trigger. Adieu, Jack, we must meet at night. Odds bottles and glasses! you shall give me a dozen bumpers to little Lydia.

ABSOLUTE
That I will with all my heart. *Exit* ACRES

322 *night . . . you shall* 1775 (night, when you shall 1776)
323 *bumpers* glasses full to the brim; hence, toasts

---

304 *according to the sentiment* as an echo to their feelings, so that if belligerent, they would swear by Mars, if amorous, by Venus
306 *echo to the sense* cf. Pope, *An Essay on Criticism,* l. 356: 'The *sound* must seem an *Eccho* to the sense'
307 *sentimental* a vogue word; here both as the adjective of 'sentiment' (l. 304), and in the sense of exhibiting refined and genteel feelings

ABSOLUTE

Now for a parental lecture—I hope he has heard nothing of the business that has brought me here. I wish the gout had held him fast in Devonshire, with all my soul!

*Enter* SIR ANTHONY

Sir, I am delighted to see you here; and looking so well!—your sudden arrival at Bath made me apprehensive for your health.

SIR ANTHONY

Very apprehensive, I dare say, Jack. What, you are recruiting here, hey?

ABSOLUTE

Yes, Sir, I am on duty.

SIR ANTHONY

Well, Jack, I am glad to see you, though I did not expect it, for I was going to write to you on a little matter of business. Jack, I have been considering that I grow old and infirm, and shall probably not trouble you long.

ABSOLUTE

Pardon me, Sir, I never saw you look more strong and hearty; and I pray frequently that you may continue so.

SIR ANTHONY

I hope your prayers may be heard with all my heart. Well then, Jack, I have been considering that I am so strong and hearty, I may continue to plague you a long time. Now, Jack, I am sensible that the income of your commission, and what I have hitherto allowed you, is but a small pittance for a lad of your spirit.

ABSOLUTE

Sir, you are very good.

SIR ANTHONY

And it is my wish, while yet I live, to have my boy make some figure in the world. I have resolved, therefore, to fix you at once in a noble independence.

ABSOLUTE

Sir, your kindness overpowers me—such generosity

---

344-5 *small pittance* If Jack's income from the army is about £190 a year (see I.i, 43), his total income, with the £50 a year that his father gives him (III. i, 16), is about the lowest level that a gentleman could manage to live on, allowing for the expenses of dress, a servant, and social life. See John Burnett, *A History of the Cost of Living* (Harmondsworth, 1969), ch. 3, and Pat Rogers, ed., *The Context of English Literature: the Eighteenth Century* (London, 1978), p. 52

makes the gratitude of reason more lively than the sensations even of filial affection.

SIR ANTHONY

I am glad you are so sensible of my attention—and you shall be master of a large estate in a few weeks.

ABSOLUTE

Let my future life, Sir, speak my gratitude: I cannot express the sense I have of your munificence.—Yet, Sir, I presume you would not wish me to quit the army?

SIR ANTHONY

Oh, that shall be as your wife chooses.

ABSOLUTE

My wife, Sir!

SIR ANTHONY

Aye, aye, settle that between you—settle that between you.

ABSOLUTE

A *wife,* Sir, did you say?

SIR ANTHONY

Aye, a wife—why, did not I mention her before?

ABSOLUTE

Not a word of her, Sir.

SIR ANTHONY

Odso!—I mustn't forget her though. Yes, Jack, the independence I was talking of is by a marriage—the fortune is saddled with a wife—but I suppose that makes no difference.

ABSOLUTE

Sir! Sir!—you amaze me!

SIR ANTHONY

Why, what the devil's the matter with the fool? Just now you were all gratitude and duty.

ABSOLUTE

I was, Sir—you talked to me of independence and a fortune, but not a word of a wife.

SIR ANTHONY

Why—what difference does that make? Odds life, Sir! if you have the estate, you must take it with the live stock on it, as it stands.

---

375 *live stock* as in his advice to 'keep a tight hand' on Lydia (as with a horse), Sir Anthony here assimilates woman to domestic animals. Compare Steele's *The Conscious Lovers*, ed. S. S. Kenny (London, 1968), p. 61, where Cimberton, the odious suitor, says that the 'better sort of people' consider marriage purely as a legal matter, 'and the woman in the bargain, like the mansion house in the sale of the estate, is thrown in'.

ABSOLUTE

If my happiness is to be the price, I must beg leave to decline the purchase. Pray, Sir, who is the lady?

SIR ANTHONY

What's that to you, Sir? Come, give me your promise to love, and to marry her directly.

ABSOLUTE

Sure, Sir, this is not very reasonable, to summon my affections for a lady I know nothing of!

SIR ANTHONY

I am sure, Sir, 'tis more unreasonable in you to *object* to a lady you know nothing of.

ABSOLUTE

Then, Sir, I must tell you plainly, that my inclinations are fixed on another—my heart is engaged to an angel.

SIR ANTHONY

Then pray let it send an excuse. It is very sorry—but *business* prevents its waiting on her.

ABSOLUTE

But my vows are pledged to her.

SIR ANTHONY

Let her foreclose, Jack; let her foreclose; they are not worth redeeming: besides, you have the angel's vows in exchange, I suppose; so there can be no loss there.

ABSOLUTE

You must excuse me, Sir, if I tell you, once for all, that in this point I cannot obey you.

SIR ANTHONY

Harkee Jack; I have heard you for some time with patience—I have been cool—quite cool; but take care—you know I am compliance itself—when I am not thwarted; no one more easily led—when I have my own way; but don't put me in a frenzy.

ABSOLUTE

Sir, I must repeat it—in this I cannot obey you.

SIR ANTHONY

Now, damn me! if ever I call you Jack again while I live!

---

390-1 *not worth redeeming* Sir Anthony, with characteristic precision of language, vivifies the dead metaphor in 'pledged': Jack has given his vows as security for a loan (of 'the angel's' love); she may prevent his ever having her love as his property (i.e., in marriage) by foreclosing, because he is not keeping up the payments (of vows). Jack will thus forfeit the value of the vows he has paid, but they are no great loss.

ABSOLUTE

Nay, Sir, but hear me.

SIR ANTHONY

Sir, I won't hear a word—not a word! not one word! so give me your promise by a nod—and I'll tell you what, Jack—I mean, you dog—if you don't, by——

ABSOLUTE

What, Sir, promise to link myself to some mass of ugliness! to——

SIR ANTHONY

Zounds! sirrah! the lady shall be as ugly as I choose: she shall have a hump on each shoulder; she shall be as crooked as the Crescent; her one eye shall roll like the bull's in Cox's museum—she shall have a skin like a mummy, and the beard of a Jew—she shall be all this, sirrah!—yet I'll make you ogle her all day, and sit up all night to write sonnets on her beauty.

ABSOLUTE

This is reason and moderation indeed!

SIR ANTHONY

None of your sneering, puppy! no grinning, jackanapes!

ABSOLUTE

Indeed, Sir, I never was in a worse humour for mirth in my life.

SIR ANTHONY

'Tis false, Sir! I know you are laughing in your sleeve: I know you'll grin when I am gone, sirrah!

ABSOLUTE

Sir, I hope I know my duty better.

SIR ANTHONY

None of your passion, Sir! none of your violence! if you please. It won't do with me, I promise you.

ABSOLUTE

Indeed, Sir, I never was cooler in my life.

SIR ANTHONY

'Tis a confounded lie! I know you are in a passion in your heart; I know you are, you hypocritical young dog! but it won't do.

416 *jackanapes* a monkey; hence, a coxcomb

---

410 *the Crescent* Royal Crescent in Bath, an architectural innovation, built 1767-74 by the younger John Wood

411 *Cox's museum* James Cox, a jeweller, had exhibited his collections of expensive adult 'toys' and ornaments, among which were various bulls, in Spring Gardens. See *Hibernian Magazine* (Dublin, 1772), II, 205-10

ABSOLUTE

Nay, Sir, upon my word.

SIR ANTHONY

So you will fly out! Can't you be cool, like me? What the devil good can *passion* do! *Passion* is of no service, you impudent, insolent, overbearing reprobate! There you sneer again!—don't provoke me!—but you rely upon the mildness of my temper—you do, you dog! you play upon the meekness of my disposition! Yet take care—the patience of a saint may be overcome at last!—but mark! I give you six hours and a half to consider of this: if you then agree, without any condition, to do everything on earth that I choose, why—confound you! I may in time forgive you—If not, zounds! don't enter the same hemisphere with me! don't dare to breathe the same air, or use the same light with me; but get an atmosphere and a sun of your own! I'll strip you of your commission; I'll lodge a five and threepence in the hands of trustees, and you shall live on the interest. I'll disown you, I'll disinherit you, I'll unget you! And damn me, if ever I call you Jack again!

*Exit* SIR ANTHONY

ABSOLUTE

Mild, gentle, considerate father—I kiss your hands. What a tender method of giving his opinion in these matters Sir Anthony has! I dare not trust him with the truth. I wonder what old, wealthy hag it is that he wants to bestow on me!—yet he himself married for love, and was in his youth a bold intriguer, and a gay companion!

*Enter* FAG

FAG

Assuredly, Sir, our father is wrath to a degree; he comes down stairs eight or ten steps at a time—muttering, growling, and thumping the banisters all the way: I, and the cook's dog, stand bowing at the door—rap! he gives me a stroke on the head with his cane; bids me carry that to my master, then kicking the poor turnspit into the area,

443 *five and threepence* a quarter of a guinea

445 *unget* i.e., un-beget

457 *turnspit* Wood notes that the people of Bath were very fond of dogs, and used them to turn their kitchen spits instead of 'poor Industrious Boys', who would be paid by licking up the dripping (op. cit., II, 416)

damns us all, for a puppy triumvirate!—Upon my credit, Sir, were I in your place, and found my father such very bad company, I should certainly drop his acquaintance.

ABSOLUTE

Cease your impertinence, Sir, at present. Did you come in for nothing more? Stand out of the way!

*Pushes him aside, and exit*

FAG

So! Sir Anthony trims my master; he is afraid to reply to his father—then vents his spleen on poor Fag! When one is vexed by one person, to revenge oneself on another, who happens to come in the way—is the vilest injustice! Ah! it shows the worst temper—the basest——

*Enter* ERRAND BOY

ERRAND BOY

Mr Fag! Mr Fag! your master calls you.

FAG

Well, you little, dirty puppy, you need not bawl so!—The meanest disposition! the——

ERRAND BOY

Quick, quick, Mr Fag.

FAG

*Quick, quick,* you impudent jackanapes! Am I to be commanded by you too? You little, impertinent, insolent, kitchen-bred—— *Exit, kicking and beating him*

458 *triumvirate* three men ruling jointly
463 *trims* reproves, scolds

## [Act II,] Scene ii

*[Scene,]* *the North Parade*
*Enter* LUCY

LUCY
So—I shall have another rival to add to my mistress's list—Captain Absolute.—However, I shall not enter his name till my purse has received notice in form. Poor Acres is dismissed! Well, I have done him a last friendly office, in letting him know that Beverley was here before him. Sir Lucius is generally more punctual when he expects to hear from his *dear Dalia*, as he calls her: I wonder he's not here! I have a little scruple of conscience from this deceit; though I should not be paid so well, if my hero knew that Delia was near fifty, and her own mistress.

*Enter* SIR LUCIUS O'TRIGGER

SIR LUCIUS
Hah! my little embassadress—upon my conscience I have been looking for you; I have been on the South Parade this half-hour.

LUCY (*Speaking simply*)
O gemini! and I have been waiting for your worship here on the North.

SIR LUCIUS
Faith!—maybe that was the reason we did not meet; and it is very comical too, how you could go out and I not see you—for I was only taking a nap at the Parade coffee-house, and I chose the window on purpose that I might not miss you.

LUCY
My stars! Now I'd wager a sixpence I went by while you were asleep.

SIR LUCIUS
Sure enough it must have been so—and I never dreamt it was so late, till I waked. Well, but my little girl, have you got nothing for me?

LUCY
Yes, but I have—I've got a letter for you in my pocket.

SIR LUCIUS
O faith! I guessed you weren't come empty-handed —well—let me see what the dear creature says.

3 *in form* according to the prescribed method (i.e., by bribing her)

LUCY

There, Sir Lucius. *Gives him a letter*

SIR LUCIUS

(*Reads*) *Sir—there is often a sudden incentive impulse in love, that has a greater induction than years of domestic combination: such was the commotion I felt at the first superfluous view of Sir Lucius O'Trigger.* Very pretty, upon my word. *Female punctuation forbids me to say more; yet let me add, that it will give me joy infallible to find Sir Lucius worthy the last criterion of my affections.—Delia.* Upon my conscience! Lucy, your lady is a great mistress of language. Faith, she's quite the queen of the dictionary!—for the devil a word dare refuse coming at her call—though one would think it was quite out of hearing.

LUCY

Aye, Sir, a lady of her experience.

SIR LUCIUS

Experience! What, at seventeen?

LUCY

O true, Sir—but then she reads so—my stars! how she will read off-hand!

SIR LUCIUS

Faith, she must be very deep read to write this way—though she is a rather arbitrary writer too—for here are a great many poor words pressed into the service of this note, that would get their *habeas corpus* from any court in Christendom.—However, when affection guides the pen, Lucy, he must be a brute who finds fault with the style.

LUCY

Ah! Sir Lucius, if you were to hear how she talks of you!

SIR LUCIUS

O tell her, I'll make her the best husband in the world, and Lady O' Trigger into the bargain! But we must get the old

30 *incentive* provocative, arousing
31 *induction* in a strained sense, an introductory process; or for, inducement
32 *commotion* for, emotion?
32 *superfluous* for, superficial
34 *punctuation* for, punctilio
35 *infallible* possibly in the sense of 'certain'; or for, ineffable
44 *off-hand* straight off
47 *pressed* forcibly enlisted, as by the press-gang
48 *habeas corpus* release (from the opening words of a writ which prevents a person being imprisoned without charge)
49-50 *However, when affection . . . the style* 1775 (omitted 1776)

gentlewoman's consent—and do everything fairly.

LUCY

Nay, Sir Lucius, I thought you wa'n't rich enough to be so nice!

SIR LUCIUS

Upon my word, young woman, you have hit it: I am so poor that I can't afford to do a dirty action. If I did not want money I'd steal your mistress and her fortune with a great deal of pleasure.—However, my pretty girl, (*Gives her money*) here's a little something to buy you a riband; and meet me in the evening, and I'll give you an answer to this. So, hussy, take a kiss beforehand, to put you in mind.

*Kisses her*

LUCY

O Lud! Sir Lucius—I never seed such a gemman! My lady won't like you if you're so impudent.

SIR LUCIUS

Faith she will, Lucy—that same—pho! what's the name of it?—modesty!—is a quality in a lover more praised by the women than liked; so, if your mistress asks you whether Sir Lucius ever gave you a kiss, tell her *fifty*—my dear.

LUCY

What, would you have me tell her a lie?

SIR LUCIUS

Ah then, you baggage! I'll make it a truth presently.

LUCY

For shame now; here is someone coming.

SIR LUCIUS

O faith, I'll quiet your conscience!

*Sees* FAG. *Exit* [SIR LUCIUS], *humming a tune*

*Enter* FAG

FAG

So, so, Ma'am. I humbly beg pardon.

LUCY

O Lud!—now, Mr Fag, you flurry one so.

FAG

Come, come, Lucy, here's no one by—so a little less simplicity, with a grain or two more sincerity, if you please.—You play false with us, Madam. I saw you give the Baronet a letter. My master shall know this—and if he doesn't call him out—I will.

56 *nice* particular, fastidious, scrupulous
71 *presently* without delay
80 *call him out* i.e., to a duel

LUCY

Ha! ha! ha! you gentlemen's gentlemen are so hasty. That letter was from Mrs Malaprop, simpleton. She is taken with Sir Lucius's address.

FAG

What tastes some people have! Why I suppose I have walked by her window an hundred times.—But what says our young lady? Any message to my master?

LUCY

Sad news! Mr Fag. A worse rival than Acres! Sir Anthony Absolute has proposed his son.

FAG

What, Captain Absolute?

LUCY

Even so—I overheard it all.

FAG

Ha! ha! ha!—very good, faith. Goodbye, Lucy, I must away with this news.

LUCY

Well—you may laugh—but it is true, I assure you. (*Going*) But, Mr Fag, tell your master not to be cast down by this.

FAG

Oh, he'll be so disconsolate!

LUCY

And charge him not to think of quarrelling with young Absolute.

FAG

Never fear!—never fear!

LUCY

Be sure—bid him keep up his spirits.

FAG

We will—we will. *Exeunt severally*

83 *address* way of behaving
84 *What tastes* 1775 (How! what tastes 1776)

## Act III, Scene i

[*Scene,*] *the North Parade*
*Enter* ABSOLUTE

ABSOLUTE
'Tis just as Fag told me, indeed. Whimsical enough, faith! My father wants to force me to marry the very girl I am plotting to run away with! He must not know of my connection with her yet awhile.—He has too summary a method of proceeding in these matters—and Lydia shall not yet lose her hopes of an elopement.—However, I'll read my recantation instantly. My conversion is something sudden, indeed, but I can assure him it is very *sincere*.—So, so—here he comes. He looks plaguy gruff. *Steps aside*

*Enter* SIR ANTHONY

SIR ANTHONY
No—I'll die sooner than forgive him. *Die*, did I say? I'll live these fifty years to plague him.—At our last meeting, his impudence had almost put me out of temper. An obstinate, passionate, self-willed boy! Who can he take after? This is my return for getting him before all his brothers and sisters!—for putting him, at twelve years old, into a marching regiment, and allowing him fifty pounds a year, besides his pay ever since! But I have done with him—he's anybody's son for me.—I never will see him more—never—never—never—never.

ABSOLUTE
Now for a penitential face. [*Advances*]

SIR ANTHONY
Fellow, get out of my way.

ABSOLUTE
Sir, you see a penitent before you.

SIR ANTHONY
I see an impudent scoundrel before me.

ABSOLUTE
A sincere penitent.—I am come, Sir, to acknowledge my

5-6 *and Lydia . . . an elopement* 1775 (omitted 1776)
14 *getting* i.e., begetting

19 *never—never—never—never* cf. *King Lear*, V. iii, 308.

error, and to submit entirely to your will.

SIR ANTHONY
What's that?

ABSOLUTE
I have been revolving, and reflecting, and considering on your past goodness, and kindness, and condescension to me.

SIR ANTHONY
Well, Sir?

ABSOLUTE
I have likewise been weighing and balancing what you were pleased to mention concerning duty, and obedience, and authority.

SIR ANTHONY
Well, puppy?

ABSOLUTE
Why then, Sir, the result of my reflections is—a resolution to sacrifice every inclination of my own to your satisfaction.

SIR ANTHONY
Why now, you talk sense—absolute sense—I never heard anything more sensible in my life.—Confound you; you shall be *Jack* again.

ABSOLUTE
I am happy in the appellation.

SIR ANTHONY
Why, then, Jack, my dear Jack, I will now inform you who the lady really is.—Nothing but your passion and violence, you silly fellow, prevented my telling you at first. Prepare, Jack, for wonder and rapture—prepare. What think you of Miss Lydia Languish?

ABSOLUTE
Languish! What, the Languishes of Worcestershire?

SIR ANTHONY
Worcestershire! No. Did you never meet Mrs Malaprop and her niece, Miss Languish, who came into our country just before you were last ordered to your regiment?

ABSOLUTE
Malaprop! Languish! I don't remember ever to have heard the names before. Yet, stay—I think I do recollect something.—Languish! Languish! She squints, don't she? A little, red-haired girl?

28 *condescension* kindness to an inferior (i.e., his son); nicely balanced between a laudatory and a pejorative sense

SIR ANTHONY

Squints? A red-haired girl! Zounds, no.

ABSOLUTE

Then I must have forgot; it can't be the same person.

SIR ANTHONY

Jack! Jack! what think you of blooming, love-breathing seventeen?

ABSOLUTE

As to that, Sir, I am quite indifferent. If I can please you in the matter, 'tis all I desire.

SIR ANTHONY

Nay, but Jack, such eyes! such eyes! so innocently wild! so bashfully irresolute! Not a glance but speaks and kindles some thought of love! Then, Jack, her cheeks! her cheeks, Jack! so deeply blushing at the insinuations of her tell-tale eyes! Then, Jack, her lips! O Jack, lips smiling at their own discretion; and if not smiling, more sweetly pouting; more lovely in sullenness!

ABSOLUTE [*Aside*]

That's she indeed. Well done, old gentleman!

SIR ANTHONY

Then, Jack, her neck. O Jack! Jack!

ABSOLUTE

And which is to be mine, Sir, the niece or the aunt?

SIR ANTHONY

Why, you unfeeling, insensible puppy, I despise you. When I was of your age, such a description would have made me fly like a rocket! The *aunt*, indeed! Odds life! when I ran away with your mother, I would not have touched anything old or ugly to gain an empire.

ABSOLUTE

Not to please your father, Sir?

SIR ANTHONY

To please my father! Zounds! not to please—O my father!—odso!—yes—yes! if my father indeed had desired—that's quite another matter. Though he wa'n't the indulgent father that I am, Jack.

ABSOLUTE

I dare say not, Sir.

SIR ANTHONY

But, Jack, you are not sorry to find your mistress is so beautiful.

69 *neck* visible part of the chest
73 *rocket* firework

ABSOLUTE

Sir, I repeat it; if I please you in this affair, 'tis all I desire. Not that I think a woman the worse for being handsome; but, Sir, if you please to recollect, you before hinted something about a hump or two, one eye, and a few more graces of that kind—now, without being very nice, I own I should rather choose a wife of mine to have the usual number of limbs, and a limited quantity of back: and though *one* eye may be very agreeable, yet as the prejudice has always run in favour of *two*, I would not wish to affect a singularity in that article.

SIR ANTHONY

What a phlegmatic sot it is! Why, sirrah, you're an anchorite!—a vile insensible stock. You a soldier!—you're a walking block, fit only to dust the company's regimentals on—odds life! I've a great mind to marry the girl myself.

ABSOLUTE

I am entirely at your disposal, Sir; if you should think of addressing Miss Languish yourself, I suppose you would have me marry the aunt; or if you should change your mind, and take the old lady—'tis the same to me—I'll marry the niece.

SIR ANTHONY

Upon my word, Jack, thou'rt either a very great hypocrite, or—but come, I know your indifference on such a subject must be all a lie—I'm sure it must—come, now—damn your demure face!—come, confess, Jack—you have been lying—ha'n't you? You have been playing the hypocrite, hey!—I'll never forgive you, if you ha'n't been lying and playing the hypocrite.

ABSOLUTE

I'm sorry, Sir, that the respect and duty which I bear to you should be so mistaken.

SIR ANTHONY

Hang your respect and duty! But, come along with me, I'll write a note to Mrs Malaprop, and you shall visit the lady directly.

ABSOLUTE

Where does she lodge, Sir?

94 *anchorite* hermit
95 *stock* block of wood
96 *block* piece of wood used as a tailor's dummy, e.g., to brush dress uniforms ('regimentals') on

---

93 *singularity* Jack puns on the senses of 'singleness' and 'extraordinariness'

SIR ANTHONY

What a dull question!—only on the Grove here.

ABSOLUTE

Oh! then I can call on her in my way to the coffee-house.

SIR ANTHONY

In your way to the coffee-house! You'll set your heart down in your way to the coffee-house, hey? Ah! you leaden-nerved, wooden-hearted dolt! But come along, you shall see her directly; her eyes shall be the Promethean torch to you—come along, I'll never forgive you, if you don't come back, stark mad with rapture and impatience—if you don't, egad, I'll marry the girl myself! *Exeunt*

## [Act III,] Scene ii

[*Scene*,] JULIA'*s dressing-room*
FAULKLAND *solus*

FAULKLAND

They told me Julia would return directly; I wonder she is not yet come! How mean does this captious, unsatisfied temper of mine appear to my cooler judgment! Yet I know not that I indulge it in any other point: but on this one subject, and to this one object, whom I think I love beyond my life, I am ever ungenerously fretful, and madly capricious! I am conscious of it—yet I cannot correct myself! What tender, honest joy sparkled in her eyes when we met! How delicate was the warmth of her expressions! I was ashamed to appear less happy—though I had come resolved to wear a face of coolness and upbraiding. Sir Anthony's presence prevented my proposed expostulations: yet I must be satisfied that she has not been so *very* happy in my absence.—She is coming!—yes!—I know the nimbleness of her tread, when she thinks her impatient Faulkland counts the moments of her stay.

*Enter* JULIA

s.d. *solus* Latin, alone
5 *object, whom* 1775 (subject, whom 1776)
6 *capricious* subject to sudden changes; guided by feelings, even whims, rather than by any settled purpose

---

116 *Grove* Orange Grove, near Bath Abbey
121 *Promethean* in Greek myth Prometheus stole fire from the gods and gave it to man: cf. *Love's Labour's Lost,* IV. iii, 301 and 348

JULIA

I had not hoped to see you again so soon.

FAULKLAND

Could I, Julia, be contented with my first welcome—restrained as we were by the presence of a third person?

JULIA

O Faulkland, when your kindness can make me thus happy, let me not think that I discovered something of coldness in your first salutation.

FAULKLAND

'Twas but your fancy, Julia. I *was* rejoiced to see you—to see you in such health—sure I had no cause for coldness?

JULIA

Nay then, I see you have taken something ill. You must not conceal from me what it is.

FAULKLAND

Well then—shall I own to you that my joy at hearing of your health and arrival here, by your neighbour Acres, was somewhat damped, by his dwelling much on the high spirits you had enjoyed in Devonshire—on your mirth—your singing—dancing, and I know not what! For such is my temper, Julia, that I should regard every mirthful moment in your absence as a treason to constancy: the mutual tear that steals down the cheek of parting lovers is a compact, that no smile shall live there till they meet again.

JULIA

Must I never cease to tax my Faulkland with this teasing minute caprice? Can the idle reports of a silly boor weigh in your breast against my tried affection?

FAULKLAND

They have no weight with me, Julia: no, no—I am happy if you have been so—yet only say, that you did not sing with *mirth*—say that you *thought* of Faulkland in the dance.

JULIA

I never can be happy in your absence. If I wear a countenance of content, it is to show that my mind holds no doubt of my Faulkland's truth. If I seemed sad, it were to make malice triumph; and say, that I had fixed my heart on one, who left me to lament his roving, and my own credulity. Believe me, Faulkland, I mean not to upbraid

23 *I was rejoiced* a correct use of the passive in the eighteenth century, but now obsolete

36 *tax . . . with* reprove . . . for

you, when I say, that I have often dressed sorrow in smiles, lest my friends should guess whose unkindness had caused my tears.

FAULKLAND

You were ever all goodness to me. Oh, I am a brute, when I but admit a doubt of your true constancy!

JULIA

If ever, without such cause from you as I will not suppose possible, you find my affections veering but a point, may I become a proverbial scoff for levity, and base ingratitude.

FAULKLAND

Ah! Julia, that *last* word is grating to me. I would I had no title to your *gratitude*! Search your heart, Julia; perhaps what you have mistaken for love is but the warm effusion of a too thankful heart!

JULIA

For what quality must I love you?

FAULKLAND

For no quality! To regard me for any quality of mind or understanding, were only to *esteem* me. And for person—I have often wished myself deformed, to be convinced that I owed no obligation there for any part of your affection.

JULIA

Where nature has bestowed a show of nice attention in the features of a man, he should laugh at it, as misplaced. I have seen men, who in *this* vain article perhaps might rank above you; but my heart has never asked my eyes whether it were so or not.

FAULKLAND

Now this is not well from *you*, Julia—I despise person in a man. Yet if you loved me as I wish, though I were an Ethiop, you'd think none so fair.

JULIA

I see you are determined to be unkind. The contract which my poor father bound us in gives you more than a lover's privilege.

FAULKLAND

Again, Julia, you raise ideas that feed and justify my doubts. I would not have been more free—no—I am proud

55 *point* one of the divisions of the compass; here, a minute distance
58 *title* claim
63 *person* appearance

---

73 *Ethiop* a poetic usage; cf. Jeremiah xiii, 23

of my restraint—yet—yet—perhaps your high respect alone for this solemn compact has fettered your inclinations, which else had made a worthier choice. How shall I be sure, had you remained unbound in thought and promise, that I should still have been the object of your persevering love?

JULIA

Then try me now. Let us be free as strangers as to what is past: *my* heart will not feel more liberty!

FAULKLAND

There now! so hasty, Julia! so anxious to be free! If your love for me were fixed and ardent, you would not loose your hold, even though I wished it!

JULIA

Oh, you torture me to the heart! I cannot bear it.

FAULKLAND

I do not mean to distress you. If I loved you less, I should never give you an uneasy moment. But hear me. All my fretful doubts arise from this—women are not used to weigh, and separate the motives of their affections: the cold dictates of prudence, gratitude, or filial duty, may sometimes be mistaken for the pleadings of the heart.—I would not boast—yet let me say, that I have neither age, person, or character, to found dislike on; my fortune such as few ladies could be charged with indiscretion in the match.—O Julia! when *love* receives such countenance from *prudence*, nice minds will be suspicious of its birth.

JULIA

I know not whither your insinuations would tend: but as they seem pressing to insult me—I will spare you the regret of having done so.—I have given you no cause for this! *Exit in tears*

FAULKLAND

In tears! stay Julia, stay but for a moment.—The door is fastened!—Julia!—my soul—but for one moment—I hear her sobbing! 'Sdeath! what a brute am I to use her thus! Yet stay—aye—she is coming now: how little resolution there is in woman!—how a few soft words can turn them! No, faith!—she is *not* coming either. Why, Julia—my love—say but that you forgive me—come but to tell me that—now, this is being *too* resentful: stay! she *is* coming too—I thought she would—no steadiness in anything! Her going away must have been a mere trick then—she shan't see that I was hurt by it. I'll affect indifference—(*Hums a tune: then listens*)—no—zounds! she's *not* coming!–nor don't intend it, I suppose. This is not steadiness, but obstinacy! Yet I deserve it. What, after so long an absence, to quarrel with her tenderness!—'twas barbarous and unmanly! I should be ashamed to see her now. I'll wait till her just resentment is abated—and when I distress her so again, may I lose her for ever! and be linked instead to some antique virago, whose gnawing passions, and long-hoarded spleen, shall make me curse my folly half the day, and all the night! *Exit*

## [Act III,] Scene iii

[*Scene,*] MRS MALAPROP'*s lodgings*
MRS MALAPROP, *and* CAPTAIN ABSOLUTE

MRS MALAPROP
Your being Sir Anthony's son, Captain, would itself be a sufficient accommodation; but from the ingenuity of your appearance, I am convinced you deserve the character here given of you.

ABSOLUTE
Permit me to say, Madam, that as I never yet have had the pleasure of seeing Miss Languish, my principal inducement in this affair at present, is the honour of being allied to Mrs Malaprop; of whose intellectual accomplishments, elegant manners, and unaffected learning, no tongue is silent.

MRS MALAPROP
Sir, you do me infinite honour! I beg, Captain, you'll be seated. ([*They*] *sit*) Ah! few gentlemen, nowadays, know how to value the ineffectual qualities in a woman! Few think how a little knowledge becomes a gentlewoman! Men have no sense now but for the worthless flower of beauty!

ABSOLUTE
It is but too true indeed, Ma'am—yet I fear our ladies

124 *virago* nagging, quarrelling woman
2 *accommodation* for, recommendation
13 *ineffectual* for, intellectual

---

2 *ingenuity* possibly in the now obsolete sense of intellectual capacity, or for ingenuousness. In either case the irony is on Mrs Malaprop for not recognizing Absolute's ingenuity (in the modern sense) in tricking her

should share the blame—they think our admiration of beauty so great, that knowledge in them would be superfluous. Thus, like garden-trees, they seldom show fruit, till time has robbed them of the more specious blossom. Few, like Mrs Malaprop and the orange-tree, are rich in both at once!

MRS MALAPROP

Sir—you overpower me with good-breeding. He is the very pineapple of politeness! You are not ignorant, Captain, that this giddy girl has somehow contrived to fix her affections on a beggarly, strolling, eavesdropping Ensign, whom none of us have seen, and nobody knows anything of.

ABSOLUTE

Oh, I have heard the silly affair before. I'm not at all prejudiced against her on that account.

MRS MALAPROP

You are very good, and very considerate, Captain. I am sure I have done everything in my power since I exploded the affair! Long ago I laid my positive conjunctions on her never to think on the fellow again—I have since laid Sir Anthony's preposition before her—but I'm sorry to say she seems resolved to decline every particle that I enjoin her.

ABSOLUTE

It must be very distressing indeed, Ma'am.

MRS MALAPROP

Oh! it gives me the hydrostatics to such a degree! I thought she had persisted from corresponding with him; but behold this very day, I have interceded another letter

27 *strolling* itinerant, vagrant
33 *exploded* possibly, discredited; or for, exposed
34 *conjunctions* for, injunctions
36 *preposition* for, proposition
37 *enjoin* command, direct
39 *hydrostatics* in eighteenth-century physics, the science of weighing fluids or bodies in fluid; for, hysterics
40 *persisted* for, desisted
41 *interceded* acted as a go-between; for, intercepted

---

25 *pineapple* for, pinnacle. Pineapple shapes were often used as architectural ornaments on the tops of pillars, towers, and so on, so that Mrs Malaprop may be said to make a wild metaphor

37 *particle* for, article; like 'conjunction' and 'preposition', a grammatical term, thus generating a pun on 'decline', in the two senses of 'refuse' and 'recite the different forms' (of a noun in inflected languages)

from the fellow! I believe I have it in my pocket.

ABSOLUTE (*Aside*)
O the devil! my last note.

MRS MALAPROP
Aye, here it is.

ABSOLUTE (*Aside*)
Aye, my note indeed! O the little traitress Lucy.

MRS MALAPROP
There, perhaps you may know the writing.
*Gives him the letter*

ABSOLUTE
I think I have seen the hand before—yes, I certainly must have seen this hand before——

MRS MALAPROP
Nay, but read it, Captain.

ABSOLUTE (*Reads*)
*My soul's idol, my adored Lydia!* Very tender indeed!

MRS MALAPROP
Tender! aye, and profane too, o' my conscience!

ABSOLUTE
*I am excessively alarmed at the intelligence you send me, the more so as my new rival——*

MRS MALAPROP
That's you, Sir.

ABSOLUTE
*has universally the character of being an accomplished gentleman, and a man of honour.* Well, that's handsome enough.

MRS MALAPROP
Oh, the fellow had some design in writing so——

ABSOLUTE
That he had, I'll answer for him, Ma'am.

MRS MALAPROP
But go on, Sir—you'll see presently.

ABSOLUTE
*As for the old weather-beaten she-dragon who guards you*—who can he mean by that?

MRS MALAPROP
*Me,* Sir—*me*—he means *me* there—what do you think now? But go on a little further.

ABSOLUTE
Impudent scoundrel!—*it shall go hard but I will elude her vigilance. as I am told that the same ridiculous vanity, which*

57 *had* 1775 (has 1776)

*makes her dress up her coarse features, and deck her dull chat with hard words which she don't understand*——

MRS MALAPROP

There, Sir! an attack upon my language! what do you think of that? An aspersion upon my parts of speech! Was ever such a brute! Sure if I reprehend anything in this world, it is the use of my oracular tongue, and a nice derangement of epitaphs!

ABSOLUTE

He deserves to be hanged and quartered! Let me see —*same ridiculous vanity*—

MRS MALAPROP

You need not read it again, Sir.

ABSOLUTE

I beg pardon, Ma'am—*does also lay her open to the grossest deceptions from flattery and pretended admiration*—an impudent coxcomb!—*so that I have a scheme to see you shortly with the old harridan's consent, and even to make her a go-between in our interviews.*—Was ever such assurance?

MRS MALAPROP

Did you ever hear anything like it? He'll elude my vigilance, will he? Yes, yes! ha! ha! He's very likely to enter these doors!—we'll try who can plot best.

ABSOLUTE

So we will Ma'am—so we will. Ha! ha! ha! a conceited puppy, ha! ha! ha! Well, but Mrs Malaprop, as the girl seems so infatuated by this fellow, suppose you were to wink at her corresponding with him for a little time—let her even plot an elopement with him—then do you connive at her escape—while *I*, just in the nick, will have the fellow laid by the heels, and fairly contrive to carry her off in his stead.

MRS MALAPROP

I am delighted with the scheme, never was anything better perpetrated!

ABSOLUTE

But, pray, could not I see the lady for a few minutes now? I should like to try her temper a little.

70 *reprehend* for, comprehend or apprehend

71 *oracular* like an oracle – i.e., speaking mysteriously and ambiguously; for, vernacular

72 *derangement* for, arrangement

72 *epitaphs* for, epithets

MRS MALAPROP

Why, I don't know—I doubt she is not prepared for a visit of this kind. There is a decorum in these matters.

ABSOLUTE

O Lord! she won't mind *me*—only tell her Beverley——

MRS MALAPROP

Sir!

ABSOLUTE (*Aside*)

Gently, good tongue.

MRS MALAPROP

What did you say of Beverley?

ABSOLUTE

Oh, I was going to propose that you should tell her, by way of jest, that it was Beverley who was below—she'd come down fast enough then—ha! ha! ha!

MRS MALAPROP

'Twould be a trick she well deserves—besides you know the fellow tells her he'll get my consent to see her—ha! ha! Let him if he can, I say again. (*Calling*) Lydia, come down here! He'll make me a *go-between in their interviews*!—ha! ha! ha! Come down, I say, Lydia! I don't wonder at your laughing, ha! ha! ha! his impudence is truly ridiculous.

ABSOLUTE

'Tis very ridiculous, upon my soul, Ma'am, ha! ha! ha!

MRS MALAPROP

The little hussy won't hear. Well, I'll go and tell her at once who it is—she shall know that Captain Absolute is come to wait on her. And I'll make her behave as becomes a young woman.

ABSOLUTE

As you please, Ma'am.

MRS MALAPROP

For the present, Captain, your servant—oh! you've not done laughing yet, I see—*elude my vigilance*! Yes, yes, ha! ha! ha! *Exit*

ABSOLUTE

Ha! ha! ha! one would think now that I might throw off all disguise at once, and seize my prize with security—but such is Lydia's caprice, that to undeceive her were probably to lose her. I'll see whether she knows me.

(*Walks aside, and seems engaged in looking at the pictures*)

*Enter* LYDIA

LYDIA

What a scene am I now to go through! Surely nothing can be more dreadful than to be obliged to listen to the loathsome addresses of a stranger to one's heart. I have heard of girls persecuted as I am, who have appealed in behalf of their favoured lover to the generosity of his rival: suppose I were to try it—there stands the hated rival—an officer too!—but oh, how unlike my Beverley!—I wonder he don't begin—truly he seems a very negligent wooer! Quite at his ease, upon my word! I'll speak first—Mr Absolute.

ABSOLUTE

Madam. *Turns round*

LYDIA

O heavens! Beverley!

ABSOLUTE

Hush!—hush, my life!—softly! be not surprised!

LYDIA

I am so astonished! and so terrified! and so overjoyed! For heaven's sake! how came you here?

ABSOLUTE

Briefly—I have deceived your aunt—I was informed that my new rival was to visit here this evening, and contriving to have him kept away, have passed myself on her for Captain Absolute.

LYDIA

O charming! And she really takes you for young Absolute?

ABSOLUTE

Oh, she's convinced of it.

LYDIA

Ha! ha! ha! I can't forbear laughing to think how her sagacity is overreached!

ABSOLUTE

But we trifle with our precious moments—such another opportunity may not occur—then let me now conjure my kind, my condescending angel, to fix the time when I may rescue her from undeserved persecution, and with a licensed warmth plead for my reward.

LYDIA

Will you then, Beverley, consent to forfeit that portion of my paltry wealth—that burden on the wings of love?

140-1 *passed myself. . . Absolute* tricked her into believing that I am Captain Absolute

150 *licensed* permitted (i.e., by marriage)

ABSOLUTE

Oh, come to me—rich only thus—in loveliness—bring no portion to me but thy love—'twill be generous in you, Lydia—for well you know, it is the only dower your poor Beverley can repay.

LYDIA

How persuasive are his words! How charming will poverty be with him!

ABSOLUTE

Ah! my soul, what a life will we then live? Love shall be our idol and support! We will worship him with a monastic strictness; abjuring all worldly toys, to centre every thought and action there. Proud of calamity, we will enjoy the wreck of wealth; while the surrounding gloom of adversity shall make the flame of our pure love show doubly bright.—By heavens! I would fling all goods of fortune from me with a prodigal hand to enjoy the scene where I might clasp my Lydia to my bosom, and say, the world affords no smile to me—but here—(*Embracing her*). (*Aside*) If she holds out now the devil is in it!

LYDIA

Now could I fly with him to the Antipodes! but my persecution is not yet come to a crisis.

*Enter* MRS MALAPROP, *listening*

MRS MALAPROP

I'm impatient to know how the little hussy deports herself.

ABSOLUTE

So pensive, Lydia!—is then your warmth abated?

MRS MALAPROP

*Warmth abated*!—so!—she has been in a passion, I suppose.

LYDIA

No—nor ever can while I have life.

MRS MALAPROP

An ill-tempered little devil! She'll be in a passion all her life, will she?

LYDIA

Think not the idle threats of my ridiculous aunt can ever have any weight with me.

161 *toys* things of no importance

---

171 s.d. *Enter* MRS MALAPROP, *listening* Mrs Malaprop misunderstands what she hears of Lydia's and Absolute's conversation like Aunt Tipkin in Steele's *The Tender Husband* (1705), III. ii

MRS MALAPROP

Very dutiful, upon my word!

LYDIA

Let her choice be Captain Absolute, but Beverley is mine.

MRS MALAPROP

I am astonished at her assurance!—to his face!—this to his face!

ABSOLUTE (*Kneeling*)

Thus then let me enforce my suit.

MRS MALAPROP

Aye—poor young man!—down on his knees entreating for pity!—I can contain no longer.—[*Reveals herself*] Why thou vixen!—I have overheard you.

ABSOLUTE (*Aside*)

Oh, confound her vigilance!

MRS MALAPROP

Captain Absolute—I know not how to apologize for her shocking rudeness.

ABSOLUTE (*Aside*)

So—all's safe, I find.—I have hopes, Madam, that time will bring the young lady——

MRS MALAPROP

Oh there's nothing to be hoped for from her! She's as headstrong as an allegory on the banks of Nile.

LYDIA

Nay, Madam, what do you charge me with now?

MRS MALAPROP

Why, thou unblushing rebel—didn't you tell this gentleman to his face that you loved another better? Didn't you say you never would be his?

LYDIA

No, Madam—I did not.

MRS MALAPROP

Good heavens! what assurance! Lydia, Lydia, you ought to know that lying don't become a young woman! Didn't you boast that Beverley—that stroller Beverley, possessed your heart? Tell me that, I say.

183 *this to his face* 1775 (this is to his face 1776)

---

195 *allegory* for, alligator (the Egyptian variety is properly called the crocodile). As Tom Moore pointed out in his *Memoirs* of Sheridan, Mrs Malaprop achieves a wild appropriateness here: 'the luckiness of her simile . . . will be acknowledged as long as there are writers to be run away with, by the wilfulness of this truly "headstrong" species of composition' (ed. cit., I, 142)

LYDIA
'Tis true, Ma'am, and none but Beverley——

MRS MALAPROP
Hold; hold Assurance! you shall not be so rude.

ABSOLUTE
Nay, pray Mrs Malaprop, don't stop the young lady's speech: she's very welcome to talk thus—it does not hurt *me* in the least, I assure you.

MRS MALAPROP
You are *too* good, Captain—*too* amiably patient—but come with me, Miss—let us see you again soon, Captain—remember what we have fixed.

ABSOLUTE
I shall, Ma'am.

MRS MALAPROP
Come, take a graceful leave of the gentleman.

LYDIA
May every blessing wait on my Beverley, my loved Bev——

MRS MALAPROP
Hussy! I'll choke the word in your throat! Come along—come along.

*Exeunt severally,* [ABSOLUTE] *kissing his hand to* LYDIA, MRS MALAPROP *stopping her from speaking*

206 *Assurance* for Mrs Malaprop, Lydia personifies assurance, in the bad sense of 'impudence'

## [Act III,] Scene iv

*[Scene,]* ACRES*'s lodgings*
ACRES *as just dressed and* DAVID

ACRES
Indeed, David—do you think I become it so?

DAVID
You are quite another creature, believe me Master, by the mass! An' we've any luck we shall see the Devon monkeyrony in all the print-shops in Bath!

ACRES
Dress *does* make a difference, David.

DAVID
'Tis all in all, I think—difference! Why, an' you were to go now to Clod Hall, I am certain the old lady wouldn't know you: Master Butler wouldn't believe his own eyes, and Mrs Pickle would cry, 'Lard presarve me!'. Our dairymaid would come giggling to the door, and I warrant Dolly Tester, your honour's favourite, would blush like my waistcoat. Oons! I'll hold a gallon, there an't a dog in the house but would bark, and I question whether Phillis would wag a hair of her tail!

ACRES
Aye, David, there's nothing like *polishing.*

DAVID
So I says of your honour's boots; but the boy never heeds me!

ACRES
But, David, has Mr De-la-Grace been here? I must rub up

1 *I become it so* i.e., my fashionable new clothes and hair-do suit me so much
3 *An'* if (dialect usage)
3 *monkeyrony* fop; a portmanteau word from 'monkey' (as a term of contempt) and 'macaroni', contemporary slang for an affected young man
11 *Tester* canopy over a bed; Dolly is presumably a chambermaid
12 *Oons* zounds (dialect form)
12 *hold a gallon* wager a gallon (of ale)

---

4 *print-shops* which sold prints and engravings – views, or likenesses of famous or fashionable people
15 *polishing* in the metaphorical sense of making or becoming elegant, which David (like the coachman) applies to his work as a servant
18 *De-la-Grace* another typifying name, 'of poise'

my balancing, and chasing, and boring.

DAVID

I'll call again, Sir.

ACRES

Do—and see if there are any letters for me at the post-office.

DAVID

I will.—By the mass, I can't help looking at your head! If I hadn't been by at the cooking, I wish I may die if I should have known the dish again myself! *Exit*

ACRES *comes forward, practising a dancing step*

ACRES

Sink, slide—coupee—confound the first inventors of cotillons! say I—they are as bad as algebra to us country gentlemen—I can walk a minuet easy enough when I'm forced!—and I have been accounted a good stick in a country dance. Odds jigs and tabors! I never valued your cross over to couple—figure in—right and left—and I'd foot it with e'er a captain in the county!—but these outlandish heathen allemandes and cotillons are quite beyond me!—I shall never prosper at 'em, that's sure—mine are true-born English legs—they don't understand their cursed French lingo!—their *pas* this, and *pas* that, and *pas* t'other!—damn me, my feet don't like to be called paws! No, 'tis certain I have most antigallican toes!

19 *balancing, and chasing, and boring* movements in dancing; respectively, moving in a converse direction from one's partner, like the arms of a balance: from French *chassé*, gliding: from French *bourrée,* a dance in three-quarter time

26 *Sink, slide—coupee* further dance movements; respectively, bending the knees: stepping smoothly to one side: a complicated step in which the dancer, resting on one foot, passes the other backward or forward, making a bow to the partner

30 *valued* was worried about

31 *cross over to couple—figure in—right and left* movements in country dancing

33 *allemandes* German dances, which may include leaping

36 *pas* French, step

38 *antigallican* opposed to what is French: in the eighteenth century, France was Britain's main enemy and thought of as a source of luxury (in the bad sense), effeminacy, and general corruption: Acres's outburst is thus parallel to, for example, the Soviet press's calling rock and roll a manifestation of capitalist decadence

*Enter* SERVANT

SERVANT

Here is Sir Lucius O'Trigger to wait on you, Sir.

ACRES

Show him in.

*Enter* SIR LUCIUS

SIR LUCIUS

Mr Acres, I am delighted to embrace you.

ACRES

My dear Sir Lucius, I kiss your hands.

SIR LUCIUS

Pray, my friend, what has brought you so suddenly to Bath?

ACRES

Faith! I have followed Cupid's jack-o'-lantern, and find myself in a quagmire at last. In short, I have been very ill-used, Sir Lucius. I don't choose to mention names, but look on me as a very ill-used gentleman.

SIR LUCIUS

Pray, what is the case? I ask no names.

ACRES

Mark me, Sir Lucius, I fall as deep as need be in love with a young lady—her friends take my part—I follow her to Bath—send word of my arrival; and receive answer, that the lady is to be otherwise disposed of. This, Sir Lucius, I call being ill-used.

SIR LUCIUS

Very ill, upon my conscience. Pray, can you divine the cause of it?

ACRES

Why, there's the matter: she has another lover, one Beverley, who, I am told, is now in Bath. Odds slanders and lies! he must be at the bottom of it.

SIR LUCIUS

A rival in the case, is there? And you think he has supplanted you unfairly?

ACRES

*Unfairly*!—to be sure he has. He never could have done it fairly.

45 *jack-o'-lantern* the *ignis fatuus;* burning marsh gas by which travellers, who mistake it for a light, are led astray

---

49 *ask no names* if he did, since he also claims Lydia's love, the plot would have to take another turn

SIR LUCIUS
Then sure you know what is to be done!

ACRES
Not I, upon my soul!

SIR LUCIUS
We wear no swords here, but you understand me.

ACRES
What! fight him!

SIR LUCIUS
Aye, to be sure: what can I mean else?

ACRES
But he has given me no provocation.

SIR LUCIUS
Now, I think he has given you the greatest provocation in the world.—Can a man commit a more heinous offence against another than to fall in love with the same woman? Oh, by my soul, it is the most unpardonable breach of friendship!

ACRES
Breach of *friendship*! Aye, aye; but I have no acquaintance with this man. I never saw him in my life.

SIR LUCIUS
That's no argument at all—he has the less right then to take such a liberty.

ACRES
Gad that's true—I grow full of anger, Sir Lucius!—I fire apace! Odds hilts and blades! I find a man may have a deal of valour in him, and not know it! But couldn't I contrive to have a little right of my side?

SIR LUCIUS
What the devil signifies *right*, when your *honour* is concerned? Do you think Achilles, or my little Alexander the Great ever inquired where the right lay? No, by my soul, they drew their broadswords, and left the lazy sons of peace to settle the justice of it.

---

66 *wear no swords* Wood (op. cit., II, 411-12) says that the wearing of swords was forbidden after fights broke out between gentlemen and chairmen. Provoked by the insolence of the chairmen, the gentlemen would draw on them, and the chairmen defend themselves with their poles, to the terror of the ladies. Goldsmith, in his life of Beau Nash, dates the prohibition from a duel in which one man died and adds the supplementary reason that the swords often frightened ladies and tore their clothes (ed. cit., III, 305)

ACRES

Your words are a grenadier's march to my heart! I believe courage must be catching! I certainly do feel a kind of valour rising as it were—a kind of courage, as I may say—odds flints, pans, and triggers! I'll challenge him directly.

SIR LUCIUS

Ah, my little friend! if we had Blunderbuss Hall here—I could show you a range of ancestry, in the O'Trigger line, that would furnish the new room, every one of whom had killed his man!—For though the mansion-house and dirty acres have slipped through my fingers, I thank heaven our honour, and the family pictures, are as fresh as ever.

ACRES

O Sir Lucius! I have had ancestors too! Every man of 'em colonel or captain in the militia! Odds balls and barrels! say no more—I'm braced for it. The thunder of your words has soured the milk of human kindness in my breast! Zounds! as the man in the play says, 'I could do such deeds!'

SIR LUCIUS

Come, come, there must be no passion at all in the case—these things should always be done civilly.

ACRES

I must be in a passion, Sir Lucius—I must be in a rage—dear Sir Lucius, let me be in a rage, if you love me.—Come, here's pen and paper. (*Sits down to write*) I would the ink were red! Indite, I say, indite! How shall I begin? Odds bullets and blades! I'll write a good bold hand, however.

SIR LUCIUS

Pray compose yourself.

91 *pans* part of a firearm which holds the gunpowder

93 *Blunderbuss Hall* a blunderbuss is a firearm with a short bore which fires many slugs at once; also, a noisy blusterer

---

88 *grenadier's march* Sir Lucius's references to Alexander and Achilles remind Acres of 'The British Grenadiers', one contemporary version of which began 'Some talk of Alexander, and some of Achilles'. See Lewis Winstock, *Songs and Music of the Redcoats* (London, 1970), pp. 29-35

95 *new room* the Assembly rooms, built 1769-71 by John Wood the younger, included a ballroom, and a tea room

102 *milk of human kindness* Acres likens himself, ludicrously, to Lady Macbeth (*Macbeth*, I. iv, 14 and 44; I. vii, 54)

103-4 *do such deeds* a mangled allusion to *King Lear*, II. iv, 279 and to *Hamlet*, III. ii, 380

ACRES

Come—now shall I begin with an oath? Do, Sir Lucius, let me begin with a damme.

SIR LUCIUS

Pho! pho! do the thing *decently* and like a Christian. Begin now—[*Dictating to* ACRES] *Sir*——

ACRES

That's too civil by half.

SIR LUCIUS

*To prevent the confusion that might arise*——

ACRES

Well——

SIR LUCIUS

*From our both addressing the same lady*——

ACRES

Aye—there's the reason—[*Writing*] *same lady*—well——

SIR LUCIUS

*I shall expect the honour of your company*——

ACRES

Zounds! I'm not asking him to dinner.

SIR LUCIUS

Pray be easy.

ACRES

Well then, *honour of your company*.

SIR LUCIUS

*To settle our pretensions*

ACRES

Well.

SIR LUCIUS

Let me see, aye, Kingsmead Fields will do. *In Kingsmead Fields*.

ACRES

So that's done. Well, I'll fold it up presently; my own crest—a hand and dagger shall be the seal.

SIR LUCIUS

You see now this little explanation will put a stop at once to all confusion or misunderstanding that might arise between you.

ACRES

Aye, we fight to prevent any misunderstanding.

---

129 *Kingsmead Fields* Kingsmead Street, where Sheridan had lived in Bath (destroyed in World War II), looked on to the open country

SIR LUCIUS

Now, I'll leave you to fix your own time. Take my advice, and you'll decide it this evening if you can; then let the worst come of it, 'twill be off your mind tomorrow.

ACRES

Very true.

SIR LUCIUS

So I shall see nothing more of you, unless it be by letter, till the evening. I would do myself the honour to carry your message; but, to tell you a secret, I believe I shall have just such another affair on my own hands. There is a gay captain here, who put a jest on me lately, at the expense of my country, and I only want to fall in with the gentleman, to call him out.

ACRES

By my valour, I should like to see you fight first! Odds life! I should like to see you kill him, if it was only to get a little lesson.

SIR LUCIUS

I shall be very proud of instructing you.—Well for the present—but remember now, when you meet your antagonist, do everything in a mild and agreeable manner. Let your courage be as keen, but at the same time as polished as your sword. *Exeunt severally*

## Act IV, Scene i

[*Scene,*] ACRES*'s lodgings*
ACRES *and* DAVID

DAVID
Then, by the mass, Sir! I would do no such thing—ne'er a Sir Lucius O'Trigger in the kingdom should make me fight, when I wa'n't so minded. Oons! what will the old lady say, when she hears o't!

ACRES
Ah! David, if you had heard Sir Lucius!—odds sparks and flames! he would have roused your valour.

DAVID
Not he, indeed. I hates such bloodthirsty cormorants. Lookee, Master, if you'd wanted a bout at boxing, quarterstaff, or short-staff, I should never be the man to bid you cry off: but for your cursed sharps and snaps, I never knew any good come of 'em.

ACRES
But my *honour,* David, my *honour*! I must be very careful of my honour.

DAVID
Aye, by the mass! and I would be very careful of it; and I think in return my honour couldn't do less than to be very careful of *me*.

ACRES
Odds blades! David, no gentleman will ever risk the loss of his honour!

DAVID
I say then, it would be but civil in honour never to risk the loss of the gentleman.—Lookee, Master, this honour seems to me to be a marvellous false friend; aye, truly, a very courtier-like servant.—Put the case, I was a gentle-

7 *cormorants* used for people whose hunger, whether for food, or, as here, for fighting, is as insatiable as the bird's
8 *quarterstaff* long heavy pole tipped with iron, a peasant's weapon
9 *short-staff* similar smaller weapon
10 *sharps* small duelling swords
10 *snaps* pistols (from the abrupt noise of the report)
14 *by the mass* an old-fashioned, countrified oath
20 *the gentleman* 1775 (a gentleman 1776)

---

20 *this honour* David's speech is reminiscent of Falstaff's in *1 Henry IV*, V. i, 127-40

man (which, thank God, no one can say of me); well—my honour makes me quarrel with another gentleman of my acquaintance. So—we fight (pleasant enough that). Boh!—I kill him (the more's my luck). Now, pray who gets the profit of it? Why, my honour. But put the case that he kills me!—by the mass! I go to the worms, and my honour whips over to my enemy!

ACRES

No, David—in that case—odds crowns and laurels! your honour follows you to the grave.

DAVID

Now, that's just the place where I could make a shift to do without it.

ACRES

Zounds, David! you're a coward! It doesn't become my valour to listen to you. What, shall I disgrace my ancestors? Think of that, David—think what it would be to disgrace my ancestors!

DAVID

Under favour, the surest way of not disgracing them, is to keep as long as you can out of their company. Lookee now, Master, to go to them in such haste—with an ounce of lead in your brains—I should think might as well be let alone. Our ancestors are very good kind of folks; but they are the last people I should choose to have a visiting acquaintance with.

ACRES

But David, now, you don't think there is such very, very, *very* great danger, hey? Odds life! people often fight without any mischief done!

DAVID

By the mass, I think 'tis ten to one against you! Oons! here to meet some lion-headed fellow, I warrant, with his damned double-barrelled swords, and cut and thrust pistols! Lord bless us! it makes me tremble to think o't!—Those be such desperate bloody-minded weapons! Well, I never could abide 'em—from a child I never could fancy 'em! I suppose there a'n't so merciless a beast in the world as your loaded pistol!

ACRES

Zounds! I *won't* be afraid—odds fire and fury! you shan't make me afraid. Here is the challenge, and I have sent for my dear friend Jack Absolute to carry it for me.

DAVID

Aye, i'the name of mischief, let *him* be the messenger. For my part, I wouldn't lend a hand to it for the best horse in your stable. By the mass! it don't look like another letter! It is, as I may say, a designing and malicious-looking letter! And I warrant smells of gunpowder like a soldier's pouch! Oons! I wouldn't swear it mayn't go off!

ACRES

Out, you poltroon!—You ha'n't the valour of a grasshopper.

DAVID

Well, I say no more—'twill be sad news, to be sure, at Clod Hall!—but I ha' done. (*Whimpering*) How Phillis will howl when she hears of it!—aye, poor bitch, she little thinks what shooting her master's going after! And I warrant old Crop, who has carried your honour, field and road, these ten years, will curse the hour he was born.

ACRES

It won't do, David—I am determined to fight—so get along, you coward, while I'm in the mind.

*Enter* SERVANT

SERVANT

Captain Absolute, Sir.

ACRES

Oh! Show him up. *Exit* SERVANT

DAVID

Well, heaven send we be all alive this time tomorrow.

ACRES

What's that! Don't provoke me, David!

DAVID (*Whimpering*)

Goodbye, Master.

ACRES

Get along, you cowardly, dastardly, croaking raven. *Exit* DAVID

*Enter* ABSOLUTE

ABSOLUTE

What's the matter, Bob?

ACRES

A vile, sheep-hearted blockhead! If I hadn't the valour of St George and the dragon to boot——

ABSOLUTE

But what did you want with me, Bob?

ACRES

Oh!—there—— *Gives him the challenge*

ABSOLUTE (*Aside*)
*To Ensign Beverley.* So—what's going on now?—Well, what's this?

ACRES
A challenge!

ABSOLUTE
Indeed! Why, you won't fight him; will you, Bob?

ACRES
Egad but I will, Jack. Sir Lucius has wrought me to it. He has left me full of rage—and I'll fight this evening, that so much good passion mayn't be wasted.

ABSOLUTE
But what have I to do with this?

ACRES
Why, as I think you know something of this fellow, I want you to find him out for me, and give him this mortal *defiance*.

ABSOLUTE
Well, give it to me, and trust me he gets it.

ACRES
Thank you, my dear friend, my dear Jack; but it is giving you a great deal of trouble.

ABSOLUTE
Not in the least—I beg you won't mention it. No trouble in the world, I assure you.

ACRES
You are very kind. What it is to have a friend! You couldn't be my second—could you, Jack?

ABSOLUTE
Why no, Bob—not in *this* affair—it would not be quite so proper.

ACRES
Well then, I must get my friend Sir Lucius. I shall have your good wishes, however, Jack.

ABSOLUTE
Whenever he meets you, believe me.

*Enter* SERVANT

SERVANT
Sir Anthony Absolute is below, inquiring for the Captain.

---

104-5 *not be quite so proper* because Absolute is thought to be an acquaintance, or at least comrade in arms, of Beverley

ABSOLUTE

I'll come instantly.—Well, my little hero, success attend you. *Going*

ACRES

Stay—stay, Jack. If Beverley should ask you what kind of a man your friend Acres is, do tell him I am a devil of a fellow—will you, Jack?

ABSOLUTE

To be sure I shall. I'll say you are a determined dog—hey, Bob!

ACRES

Aye, do, do—and if that frightens him, egad perhaps he mayn't come. So tell him I generally kill a man a week; will you, Jack?

ABSOLUTE

I will, I will; I'll say you are called in the country 'Fighting Bob'!

ACRES

Right, right—'tis all to prevent mischief; for I don't want to take his life if I clear my honour.

ABSOLUTE

No!—that's very kind of you.

ACRES

Why, you don't wish me to kill him—do you, Jack?

ABSOLUTE

No, upon my soul, I do not. But a devil of a fellow, hey? *Going*

ACRES

True, true—but stay—stay, Jack—you may add that you never saw me in such a rage before—a most devouring rage!

ABSOLUTE

I will, I will.

ACRES

Remember, Jack—a determined dog!

ABSOLUTE

Aye, aye, 'Fighting Bob'! *Exeunt severally*

## [Act IV,] Scene ii

[*Scene,*] MRS MALAPROP*'s lodgings*
MRS MALAPROP *and* LYDIA

MRS MALAPROP
Why, thou perverse one!—tell me what you can object to him? Isn't he a handsome man? Tell me that. A genteel man? A pretty figure of a man?

LYDIA (*Aside*)
She little thinks whom she is praising!—So is Beverley, Ma'am.

MRS MALAPROP
No caparisons, Miss, if you please! Caparisons don't become a young woman. No! Captain Absolute is indeed a fine gentleman!

LYDIA (*Aside*)
Aye, the Captain Absolute *you* have seen.

MRS MALAPROP
Then he's *so* well bred—*so* full of alacrity, and adulation!—and has *so much* to say for himself: in such good language too! His physiognomy so grammatical! Then his presence is so noble! I protest, when I saw him, I thought of what Hamlet says in the play: 'Hesperian curls!—the front of Job himself!—an eye, like March, to threaten at command!—a station, like Harry Mercury, new'—something about kissing—on a hill—however, the similitude struck me directly.

LYDIA (*Aside*)
How enraged she'll be presently when she discovers her mistake!

*Enter* SERVANT

SERVANT
Sir Anthony and Captain Absolute are below Ma'am.

MRS MALAPROP
Show them up here. *Exit* SERVANT
Now, Lydia, I insist on your behaving as becomes a young

6 *caparisons* ornamental saddle-cloths; for, comparisons
10 *adulation* Mrs Malaprop misuses the word in a non-pejorative sense, to describe Absolute's pretended admiration of her
12 *physiognomy* the face as an indication of character: for, phraseology

14 *what Hamlet says* describing his father to Gertrude, *Hamlet,* III. iv, 56-9

woman. Show your good breeding at least, though you have forgot your duty.

LYDIA

Madam, I have told you my resolution; I shall not only give him no encouragement, but I won't even speak to, or look at him.

*Flings herself into a chair, with her face from the door*

*Enter* SIR ANTHONY *and* ABSOLUTE

SIR ANTHONY

Here we are, Mrs Malaprop; come to mitigate the frowns of unrelenting beauty—and difficulty enough I had to bring this fellow. I don't know what's the matter; but if I hadn't held him by force, he'd have given me the slip.

MRS MALAPROP

You have infinite trouble, Sir Anthony, in the affair. I am ashamed for the cause! (*Aside to her*) Lydia, Lydia, rise I beseech you!— pay your respects!

SIR ANTHONY

I hope, Madam, that Miss Languish has reflected on the worth of this gentleman, and the regard due to her aunt's choice, and *my* alliance. (*Aside to him*) Now, Jack, speak to her!

ABSOLUTE (*Aside*)

What the devil shall I do!—You see, Sir, she won't even look at me, whilst you are here. I knew she wouldn't! I told you so. Let me entreat you, Sir, to leave us together!

*Seems to expostulate with his father*

LYDIA (*Aside*)

I wonder I ha'n't heard my aunt exclaim yet! sure she can't have looked at him!—perhaps their regimentals are alike, and she is something blind.

SIR ANTHONY

I say, Sir, I won't stir a foot yet.

MRS MALAPROP

I am sorry to say, Sir Anthony, that my affluence over my niece is very small. (*Aside to her*) Turn round Lydia, I blush for you!

45 *something* somewhat

47 *affluence* possibly the term from contemporary science, meaning a flowing (of blood, electricity, 'phlogiston'); for, influence

---

29 *mitigate the frowns* see Introduction, p. xxv

SIR ANTHONY

May I not flatter myself that Miss Languish will assign what cause of dislike she can have to my son. (*Aside to him*) Why don't you begin, Jack? Speak, you puppy—speak!

MRS MALAPROP

It is impossible, Sir Anthony, she can have any. She will not *say* she has. (*Aside to her*) Answer, hussy! why don't you answer?

SIR ANTHONY

Then, Madam, I trust that a childish and hasty predilection will be no bar to Jack's happiness. (*Aside to him*) Zounds! sirrah! why don't you speak?

LYDIA (*Aside*)

I think my lover seems as little inclined to conversation as myself. How strangely blind my aunt must be!

ABSOLUTE

Hem! hem!—Madam—hem! (ABSOLUTE *attempts to speak, then returns to* SIR ANTHONY) Faith! Sir, I am so confounded!—and so—so—confused! I told you I should be so, Sir—I knew it—the—the—tremor of my passion, entirely takes away my presence of mind.

SIR ANTHONY

But it don't take away your voice, fool, does it? Go up, and speak to her directly!

ABSOLUTE *makes signs to* MRS MALAPROP *to leave them together*

MRS MALAPROP

Sir Anthony, shall we leave them together? (*Aside to her*) Ah! you stubborn little vixen!

SIR ANTHONY

Not yet, Ma'am, not yet! (*Aside to him*) What the devil are you at? Unlock your jaws, sirrah, or——

ABSOLUTE *draws near* LYDIA

ABSOLUTE

Now heaven send she may be too sullen to look round! (*Aside*) I must disguise my voice. (*Speaks in a low hoarse tone*) Will not Miss Languish lend an ear to the mild accents of true love? Will not——

SIR ANTHONY

What the devil ails the fellow? Why don't you speak out? —not stand croaking like a frog in a quinsy!

77 *quinsy* inflammation of the throat

ABSOLUTE

The— the— excess of my awe, and my—my—my modesty, quite choke me!

SIR ANTHONY

Ah! your *modesty* again! I'll tell you what, Jack; if you don't speak out directly, and glibly too, I shall be in such a rage! Mrs Malaprop, I wish the lady would favour us with something more than a side-front!

MRS MALAPROP *seems to chide* LYDIA

ABSOLUTE [*Aside*]

So!—all will out I see! (*Goes up to* LYDIA, *speaks softly*) Be not surprised, my Lydia, suppress all surprise at present.

LYDIA (*Aside*)

Heavens! 'tis Beverley's voice! Sure he can't have imposed on Sir Anthony too! (*Looks round by degrees, then starts up*) Is this possible!—my Beverley!—how can this be?—my Beverley?

ABSOLUTE (*Aside*)

Ah! 'tis all over.

SIR ANTHONY

Beverley!—the devil—Beverley!—What can the girl mean? This is my son, Jack Absolute!

MRS MALAPROP

For shame, hussy! for shame!—your head runs so on that fellow, that you have him always in your eyes! Beg Captain Absolute's pardon directly.

LYDIA

I see no Captain Absolute, but my loved Beverley!

SIR ANTHONY

Zounds! the girl's mad!—her brain's turned by reading!

MRS MALAPROP

O' my conscience, I believe so! What do you mean by Beverley, hussy? You saw Captain Absolute before today; there he is—your husband that shall be.

LYDIA

With all my soul, Ma'am—when I refuse my Beverley——

SIR ANTHONY

Oh! she's as mad as Bedlam!—or has this fellow been playing us a rogue's trick! Come here, sirrah! Who the devil are you?

102 *Bedlam* a corruption of Bethlehem hospital in London, an asylum for lunatics

ABSOLUTE

Faith, Sir, I am not quite clear myself; but I'll endeavour to recollect.

SIR ANTHONY

Are you my son, or not? Answer for your mother, you dog, if you won't for me.

MRS MALAPROP

Aye, Sir, who are you? O mercy! I begin to suspect——

ABSOLUTE (*Aside*)

Ye powers of impudence befriend me!—Sir Anthony, most assuredly I am your wife's son; and that I sincerely believe myself to be *yours* also, I hope my duty has always shown. Mrs Malaprop, I am your most respectful admirer—and shall be proud to add *affectionate nephew*. I need not tell my Lydia, that she sees her faithful Beverley, who, knowing the singular generosity of her temper, assumed that name, and a station, which has proved a test of the most disinterested love, which he now hopes to enjoy in a more elevated character.

LYDIA (*Sullenly*)

So!—there will be no elopement after all!

SIR ANTHONY

Upon my soul, Jack, thou art a very impudent fellow! To do you justice, I think I never saw a piece of more consummate assurance!

ABSOLUTE

Oh, you flatter me, Sir—you compliment—'tis my *modesty* you know, Sir—my modesty that has stood in my way.

SIR ANTHONY

Well, I am glad you are not the dull, insensible varlet you pretended to be, however! I'm glad you have made a fool of your father, you dog—I am.—So this was your penitence, your duty, and obedience! I thought it was damned sudden! You never heard their names before, not you!—What, Languishes of Worcestershire, hey?—if you could please me in the affair, 'twas all you desired! Ah! you dissembling villain! What! (*Pointing to* LYDIA) she squints, don't she?—a little red-haired girl!—hey? Why, you hypocritical young rascal—I wonder you a'n't ashamed to hold up your head!

ABSOLUTE

'Tis with much difficulty, Sir—I am confused—very much confused, as you must perceive.

118 *disinterested* unbiased (here, by mercenary considerations)

MRS MALAPROP

O Lud! Sir Anthony!—a new light breaks in upon me!—hey! how! what! Captain, did *you* write the letters then? What! I am to thank *you* for the elegant compilation of 'an old weather-beaten she-dragon'—hey? O mercy! —was it *you* that reflected on my parts of speech?

ABSOLUTE [*Aside to* SIR ANTHONY]

Dear Sir! my modesty will be overpowered at last, if you don't assist me. I shall certainly not be able to stand it!

SIR ANTHONY

Come, come, Mrs Malaprop, we must forget and forgive; odds life! matters have taken so clever a turn all of a sudden, that I could find it in my heart, to be so good-humoured! and so gallant!—hey! Mrs Malaprop!

MRS MALAPROP

Well, Sir Anthony, since you desire it, we will not anticipate the past; so mind young people—our retrospection will now be all to the future.

SIR ANTHONY

Come, we must leave them together, Mrs Malaprop; they long to fly into each other's arms, I warrant! Jack, isn't the cheek as I said, hey? And the eye, you rogue! and the lip—hey? Come, Mrs Malaprop, we'll not disturb their tenderness—theirs is the time of life for happiness! (*Sings*) 'Youth's the season made for joy'—hey! —odds life! I'm in such spirits—I don't know what I couldn't do! (*Gives his hand to* MRS MALAPROP) Permit me, Ma'am—(*Sings*) Tol-de-rol—gad I should like a little fooling myself—tol-de-rol! de-rol!

*Exit singing, and handing* MRS MALAPROP

LYDIA *sits sullenly in her chair*

ABSOLUTE (*Aside*)

So much thought bodes me no good.—So grave, Lydia!

LYDIA

Sir!

ABSOLUTE (*Aside*)

So!—egad! I thought as much!—that damned mono-

141 *I am* 1775 (am I 1776)
141 *compilation* literary work culled from various sources; for, appellation
147 *clever* convenient and agreeable
162 s.d. *handing* leading by the hand

150-2 *not anticipate . . . to the future* a self-contradictory proposition, or bull
158 *Youth's the season* see Appendix

syllable has froze me!—What, Lydia, now that we are as happy in our friends' consent as in our mutual vows——

LYDIA (*Peevishly*)

Friends' consent, indeed!

ABSOLUTE

Come, come, we must lay aside some of our romance—a little wealth and comfort may be endured after all. And for your fortune, the lawyers shall make such settlements as——

LYDIA

Lawyers! I *hate* lawyers!

ABSOLUTE

Nay then, we will not wait for their lingering forms, but instantly procure the licence, and——

LYDIA

The licence! I *hate* licence!

ABSOLUTE

O my love! Be not so unkind!—thus let me entreat ——*Kneeling*

LYDIA

Pshaw!—what signifies kneeling, when you know I *must* have you?

ABSOLUTE (*Rising*)

Nay, Madam, there shall be no constraint upon your inclinations, I promise you. If I have lost your *heart*—I resign the rest. (*Aside*) Gad, I must try what a little *spirit* will do.

LYDIA (*Rising*)

Then, Sir, let me tell you, the interest you had there was acquired by a mean, unmanly imposition, and deserves the punishment of fraud. What, you have been treating *me* like a *child*!—humouring my romance! and laughing, I suppose, at your success!

ABSOLUTE

You wrong me, Lydia, you wrong me—only hear——

LYDIA (*Walking about in heat*)

So, while I fondly imagined we were deceiving my relations, and flattered myself that I should outwit and incense them all—behold! my hopes are to be crushed at once, by my aunt's consent and approbation!—and I am myself the only dupe at last!

---

171 *settlements* perhaps to give Lydia control of her own fortune, which would otherwise become her husband's property, and thus absolve Jack from any suspicion that he loves not her but her money

ABSOLUTE

Nay, but hear me——

LYDIA

No, Sir, you could not think that such paltry artifices could please me, when the mask was thrown off! But I suppose since your tricks have made you secure of my fortune, you are little solicitous about my affections.—But here, Sir, here is the picture—Beverley's picture! (*Taking a miniature from her bosom*) which I have worn, night and day, in spite of threats and entreaties! There, Sir, (*Flings it to him*) and be assured I throw the original from my heart as easily!

ABSOLUTE

Nay, nay, Ma'am, we will not differ as to that. Here, (*Taking out a picture*) *here* is Miss Lydia Languish. What a difference!—aye, there is the heavenly assenting smile, that first gave soul and spirit to my hopes!—those are the lips which sealed a vow, as yet scarce dry in Cupid's calendar!—and there the half resentful blush, that would have checked the ardour of my thanks.—Well, all that's past!—all over indeed! There, Madam—in beauty, that copy is not equal to you, but in my mind its merit over the original, in being still the same, is such—that—I cannot find in my heart to part with it. *Puts it up again*

LYDIA (*Softening*)

'Tis your own doing, Sir—I—I—I suppose you are perfectly satisfied.

ABSOLUTE

Oh, most certainly—sure now this is much better than being in love!—ha! ha! ha!—there's some spirit in *this*! What signifies breaking some scores of solemn promises—all that's of no consequence you know. To be sure people will say, that Miss didn't know her own mind—but never mind that: or perhaps they may be ill-natured enough to hint, that the gentleman grew tired of the lady and forsook her—but don't let that fret you.

LYDIA

There's no bearing his insolence. *Bursts into tears*

*Enter* MRS MALAPROP *and* SIR ANTHONY

MRS MALAPROP (*Entering*)

Come, we must interrupt your billing and cooing a while.

195-9 *Nay, but hear me . . . about my affections* 1775 (omitted 1776)

LYDIA (*Sobbing*)

This is worse than your treachery and deceit, you base ingrate!

SIR ANTHONY

What the devil's the matter now! Zounds! Mrs Malaprop, this is the oddest *billing* and *cooing* I ever heard!—but what the deuce is the meaning of it? I'm quite astonished!

ABSOLUTE

Ask the lady, Sir.

MRS MALAPROP

O mercy!—I'm quite analysed for my part! Why, Lydia, what is the reason of this?

LYDIA

Ask the gentleman, Ma'am.

SIR ANTHONY

Zounds! I shall be in a frenzy! Why Jack, you scoundrel, you are not come out to be anyone else, are you?

MRS MALAPROP

Aye, Sir, there's no more trick, is there? You are not like Cerberus, *three* gentlemen at once, are you?

ABSOLUTE

You'll not let me speak—I say the lady can account for this much better than I can.

LYDIA

Ma'am, you once commanded me never to think of Beverley again—there is the man—I now obey you: for, from this moment, I renounce him for ever. *Exit* LYDIA

MRS MALAPROP

O mercy! and miracles! what a turn here is—why sure, Captain, you haven't behaved disrespectfully to my niece.

SIR ANTHONY

Ha! ha! ha!—ha! ha! ha!—now I see it—ha! ha! ha!—now I see it—you have been too lively, Jack.

ABSOLUTE

Nay, Sir, upon my word——

229 *ingrate* a person lacking in gratitude; Jack's coolness is the most wounding to Lydia

234 *analysed* in grammatical or scientific use, of a thing reduced to its elements; for, paralysed?

237 *you scoundrel* 1775 (omitted 1776)

240 *Cerberus* in classical mythology, the three-headed dog which guarded the entrance to the underworld; for, Proteus, a sea god who could assume various shapes

SIR ANTHONY

Come, no excuses, Jack; why, your father, you rogue, was so before you: the blood of the Absolutes was always impatient. Ha! ha! ha! poor little Lydia!—why, you've frightened her, you dog, you have.

ABSOLUTE

By all that's good, Sir——

SIR ANTHONY

Zounds! say no more, I tell you. Mrs Malaprop shall make your peace. You must make his peace, Mrs Malaprop; you must tell her 'tis Jack's way—tell her 'tis all our ways—it runs in the blood of our family! Come, get on, Jack—ha! ha! ha! Mrs Malaprop—a young villain! *Pushing him out*

MRS MALAPROP

Oh! Sir Anthony! O fie, Captain! *Exeunt severally*

## [Act IV,] Scene iii

*[Scene,] the North Parade*
*Enter* SIR LUCIUS O'TRIGGER

SIR LUCIUS

I wonder where this Captain Absolute hides himself. Upon my conscience! these officers are always in one's way in love affairs: I remember I might have married Lady Dorothy Carmine, if it had not been for a little rogue of a Major, who ran away with her before she could get a sight of me!—And I wonder too what it is the ladies can see in them to be so fond of them—unless it be a touch of the old serpent in 'em, that makes the little creatures be caught, like vipers with a bit of red cloth.—Hah!—isn't this the Captain coming? Faith it is! There is a probability of succeeding about that fellow, that is mighty provoking! Who the devil is he talking to? *Steps aside*

*Enter* CAPTAIN ABSOLUTE

ABSOLUTE

To what fine purpose I have been plotting! A noble reward for all my schemes, upon my soul!—a little gipsy! I

260 s.d. *Pushing him out* 1775 (Pushes him out 1776)
10-11 *probability of succeeding* look of success
14 *gipsy* fickle woman

8-9 *serpent . . red cloth* women tempt men, like the serpent in Genesis, and 'the old serpent', the devil. Women, 'the little creatures', are attracted by military men, in their red uniforms, as vipers were erroneously thought to be attracted by red cloth (vipers, or adders, in fact cannot distinguish colour, and unlike bees, do not expend all their poison in one bite)

did not think her romance could have made her so damned absurd either, 'Sdeath, I never was in a worse humour in my life! I could cut my own throat, or any other person's, with the greatest pleasure in the world!

SIR LUCIUS

Oh, faith! I'm in the luck of it—I never could have found him in a sweeter temper for my purpose—to be sure I'm just come in the nick! Now to enter into conversation with him, and so quarrel genteelly. (SIR LUCIUS *goes up to* ABSOLUTE) With regard to that matter, Captain, I must beg leave to differ in opinion with you.

ABSOLUTE

Upon my word then, you must be a very subtle disputant: because, Sir, I happened just then to be giving no opinion at all.

SIR LUCIUS

That's no reason. For give me leave to tell you, a man may think an untruth as well as speak one.

ABSOLUTE

Very true, Sir, but if the man never utters his thoughts, I should think they might stand a chance of escaping controversy.

SIR LUCIUS

Then, Sir, you differ in opinion with me, which amounts to the same thing.

ABSOLUTE

Harkee, Sir Lucius—if I had not before known you to be a gentleman, upon my soul, I should not have discovered it at this interview: for what you can drive at, unless you mean to quarrel with me, I cannot conceive!

SIR LUCIUS (*Bowing*)

I humbly thank you, Sir, for the quickness of your apprehension—you have named the very thing I would be at.

ABSOLUTE

Very well, Sir—I shall certainly not baulk your inclinations—but I should be glad you would please to explain your motives.

22 *genteelly* see II. i, 297

---

38 *quarrel* Sir Lucius draws Jack into agreeing to a duel by contradicting him, i.e., implying that Jack is a liar, an accusation against which his honour as a gentleman demands that he must defend himself

SIR LUCIUS

Pray, Sir, be easy—the quarrel is a very pretty quarrel as it stands—we should only spoil it, by trying to explain it. However, your memory is very short—or you could not have forgot an affront you passed on me within this week. So, no more, but name your time and place.

ABSOLUTE

Well, Sir, since you are so bent on it, the sooner the better; let it be this evening—here, by the Spring Gardens. We shall scarcely be interrupted.

SIR LUCIUS

Faith! that same interruption in affairs of this nature shows very great ill-breeding. I don't know what's the reason, but in England, if a thing of this kind gets wind, people make such a pother, that a gentleman can never fight in peace and quietness. However, if it's the same to you, Captain, I should take it as a particular kindness, if you'd let us meet in Kingsmead Fields, as a little business will call me there about six o' clock, and I may dispatch both matters at once.

ABSOLUTE

'Tis the same to me exactly. A little after six, then, we will discuss this matter more seriously.

SIR LUCIUS

If you please, Sir, there will be very pretty small-sword light, though it won't do for a long shot.—So that matter's settled! and my mind's at ease. *Exit* SIR LUCIUS

*Enter* FAULKLAND, *meeting* ABSOLUTE

ABSOLUTE

Well met—I was going to look for you. O Faulkland! all the demons of spite and disappointment have conspired against me! I'm so vexed, that if I had not the prospect of a resource in being knocked o'the head by and by, I should scarce have spirits to tell you the cause.

FAULKLAND

What can you mean? Has Lydia changed her mind? I

52 *scarcely* hardly; almost in the sense of 'not'

64 *small-sword* light sword used in fencing and duelling

70 *resource* used ironically in the sense of something which provides relaxation or amusement

---

51 *Spring Gardens* a 'sweet retreat', with gardens and a room for dancing and meals, across the river from the Grove; see *Humphrey Clinker,* ed. cit., p. 70

should have thought her duty and inclination would now have pointed to the same object.

ABSOLUTE

Aye, just as the eyes do of a person who squints: when her love eye was fixed on me—t'other, her eye of duty, was finely obliqued: but when duty bid her point that the same way—off t'other turned on a swivel, and secured its retreat with a frown!

FAULKLAND

But what's the resource you——

ABSOLUTE

Oh, to wind up the whole, a good-natured Irishman here has (*Mimicking* SIR LUCIUS) begged leave to have the pleasure of cutting my throat—and I mean to indulge him—that's all.

FAULKLAND

Prithee, be serious.

ABSOLUTE

'Tis fact, upon my soul. Sir Lucius O'Trigger—you know him by sight—for some affront, which I am sure I never intended, has obliged me to meet him this evening at six o'clock: 'tis on that account I wished to see you—you must go with me.

FAULKLAND

Nay, there must be some mistake, sure. Sir Lucius shall explain himself—and I dare say matters may be accommodated: but this evening, did you say? I wish it had been any other time.

ABSOLUTE

Why?—there will be light enough: there will (as Sir Lucius says) 'be very pretty small-sword light, though it won't do for a long shot'. Confound his long shots!

FAULKLAND

But I am myself a good deal ruffled, by a difference I have had with Julia—my vile tormenting temper had made me treat her so cruelly, that I shall not be myself till we are reconciled.

ABSOLUTE

By heavens, Faulkland, you don't deserve her.

*Enter* SERVANT, *gives* FAULKLAND *a letter* [*Exit* SERVANT]

FAULKLAND

O Jack! this is from Julia—I dread to open it—I fear it may be to take a last leave—perhaps to bid me return her letters—and restore—oh! how I suffer for my folly!

ABSOLUTE

Here—let me see. (*Takes the letter and opens it*) Aye, a final sentence indeed!—'tis all over with you, faith!

FAULKLAND

Nay, Jack—don't keep me in suspense.

ABSOLUTE

Hear then. *As I am convinced that my dear Faulkland's own reflections have already upbraided him for his last unkindness to me, I will not add a word on the subject. I wish to speak with you as soon as possible. Yours ever and truly, Julia.*—There's stubbornness and resentment for you! (*Gives him the letter*) Why, man, you don't seem one whit the happier at this.

FAULKLAND

Oh, yes, I am—but—but——

ABSOLUTE

Confound your buts. You never hear anything that would make another man bless himself, but you immediately damn it with a but.

FAULKLAND

Now, Jack, as you are my friend, own honestly—don't you think there is something forward—something indelicate in this haste to forgive? Women should never sue for reconciliation: that should *always* come from us. They should retain their coldness till wooed to kindness—and their pardon, like their love, should 'not unsought be won'.

ABSOLUTE

I have not patience to listen to you: thou'rt incorrigible!—so say no more on the subject. I must go to settle a few matters—let me see you before six—remember—at my lodgings. A poor industrious devil like me, who have toiled, and drudged, and plotted to gain my ends, and am at last disappointed by other people's folly—may in pity be allowed to swear and grumble a little; but a captious sceptic in love—a slave to fretfulness and whim—who has no difficulties but of his own creating—is a subject more fit for ridicule than compassion! *Exit* ABSOLUTE

FAULKLAND

I feel his reproaches! Yet I would not change this too exquisite nicety, for the gross content with which he tram-

122 *sue* seek

125 *not unsought be won Paradise Lost,* VIII, 503, describing Eve's 'innocence and virgin modesty'

ples on the thorns of love. His engaging me in this duel has started an idea in my head, which I will instantly pursue. I'll use it as the touchstone of Julia's sincerity and disinterestedness—if her love prove pure and sterling ore—my name will rest on it with honour! And once I've stamped it there, I lay aside my doubts for ever: but if the dross of selfishness, the allay of pride predominate—'twill be best to leave her as a toy for some less cautious fool to sigh for.

*Exit* FAULKLAND

## Act V, Scene i

[*Scene,*] JULIA'*s dressing-room*

JULIA, *sola*

JULIA

How this message has alarmed me! what dreadful accident can he mean! why such charge to be alone? O Faulkland! how many unhappy moments! how many tears have you cost me!

*Enter* FAULKLAND, *muffled up in a riding-coat*

JULIA

What means this?—Why this caution, Faulkland?

FAULKLAND

Alas! Julia, I am come to take a long farewell.

JULIA

Heavens! what do you mean?

FAULKLAND

You see before you a wretch, whose life is forfeited. Nay, start not! The infirmity of my temper has drawn all this misery on me. I left you fretful and passionate—an untoward accident drew me into a quarrel—the event is, that I must fly this kingdom instantly. O Julia, had I been so fortunate as to have called you mine entirely, before this mischance had fallen on me, I should not so deeply dread my banishment!

140 *touchstone* test, criterion
s.d. *sola* Latin, alone
2 *charge* order
4 s.d. *muffled up in a riding-coat* 1775 (omitted 1776)
11 *event* consequence
12 *O Julia* 1775 (Julia 1776)

141-4 *sterling ore . . . allay of pride* The metaphor is that of coining metal. Faulkland's name (given to Julia on their marriage) is compared to the stamp making a piece of metal good current coin; if the metal is impure or allayed with a baser metal, it is unfit for coining

JULIA

My soul is oppressed with sorrow at the nature of your misfortune: had these adverse circumstances arisen from a less fatal cause, I should have felt strong comfort in the thought that I could *now* chase from your bosom every doubt of the warm sincerity of my love. My heart has long known no other guardian—I now entrust my person to your honour—we will fly together. When safe from pursuit, my father's will may be fulfilled—and I receive a legal claim to be the partner of your sorrows, and tenderest comforter. Then on the bosom of your wedded Julia, you may lull your keen regret to slumbering; while virtuous love, with a cherub's hand, shall smooth the brow of upbraiding thought, and pluck the thorn from compunction.

FAULKLAND

O Julia! I am bankrupt in gratitude! but the time is so pressing, it calls on you for so hasty a resolution. Would you not wish some hours to weigh the advantages you forego, and what little compensation poor Faulkland can make you beside his solitary love?

JULIA

I ask not a moment. No, Faulkland, I have loved you for yourself: and if I now, more than ever, prize the solemn engagement which so long has pledged us to each other, it is because it leaves no room for hard aspersions on my fame, and puts the seal of duty to an act of love. But let us not linger—perhaps this delay——

FAULKLAND

'Twill be better I should not venture out again till dark. Yet am I grieved to think what numberless distresses will press heavy on your gentle disposition!

JULIA

Perhaps your fortune may be forfeited by this unhappy act. I know not whether 'tis so—but sure that alone can never make us unhappy. The little I have will be sufficient to support us; and exile never should be splendid.

FAULKLAND

Aye, but in such an abject state of life, my wounded pride perhaps may increase the natural fretfulness of my temper, till I become a rude, morose companion, beyond your patience to endure. Perhaps the recollection of a deed my conscience cannot justify, may haunt me in such gloomy and unsocial fits, that I shall hate the tenderness that would relieve me, break from your arms, and quarrel with your fondness!

JULIA

If your thoughts should assume so unhappy a bent, you will the more want some mild and affectionate spirit to watch over and console you: one who, by bearing your infirmities with gentleness and resignation, may teach you so to bear the evils of your fortune.

FAULKLAND

O Julia, I have proved you to the quick! and with this useless device I throw away all my doubts. How shall I plead to be forgiven this last unworthy effect of my restless, unsatisfied disposition?

JULIA

Has no such disaster happened as you related?

FAULKLAND

I am ashamed to own that it was all pretended; yet, in pity, Julia, do not kill me with resenting a fault which never can be repeated: but sealing, this once, my pardon, let me tomorrow, in the face of heaven, receive my future guide and monitress, and expiate my past folly, by years of tender adoration.

JULIA

Hold, Faulkland! That you are free from a crime, which I before feared to name, heaven knows how sincerely I rejoice! These are tears of thankfulness for that! But that your cruel doubts should have urged you to an imposition that has wrung my heart, gives me now a pang, more keen than I can express!

FAULKLAND

By heavens! Julia——

JULIA

Yet hear me.—My father loved you, Faulkland! and you preserved the life that tender parent gave me; in his presence I pledged my hand—joyfully pledged it—where before I had given my heart. When, soon after, I lost that parent, it seemed to me that providence had, in Faulkland, shown me whither to transfer, without a pause, my grateful duty, as well as my affection. Hence I have been content to bear from you what pride and delicacy would

61 *proved . . . to the quick* tested to the utmost
75 *imposition* imposture, trick

have forbid me from another. I will not upbraid you, by repeating how you have trifled with my sincerity——

FAULKLAND

I confess it all! yet hear——

JULIA

After such a year of trial—I might have flattered myself that I should not have been insulted with a new probation of my sincerity, as cruel as unnecessary! I now see it is not in your nature to be content, or confident in love. With this conviction—I never will be yours. While I had hopes that my persevering attention, and unreproaching kindness might in time reform your temper, I should have been happy to have gained a dearer influence over you; but I will not furnish you with a licensed power to keep alive an incorrigible fault, at the expense of one who never would contend with you.

FAULKLAND

Nay, but Julia, by my soul and honour, if after this——

JULIA

But one word more. As my faith has once been given to you, I never will barter it with another. I shall pray for your happiness with the truest sincerity; and the dearest blessing I can ask of heaven to send you, will be to charm you from that unhappy temper, which alone has prevented the performance of our solemn engagement. All I request of you is, that you will yourself reflect upon this infirmity, and when you number up the many true delights it has deprived you of—let it not be your *least* regret, that it lost you the love of one—who would have followed you in beggary through the world! *Exit*

FAULKLAND

She's gone!—for ever! There was an awful resolution in her manner, that riveted me to my place.—O fool! —dolt!—barbarian! Curst as I am, with more imperfections than my fellow-wretches, kind fortune sent a heaven-gifted cherub to my aid, and, like a ruffian, I have driven her from my side! I must now haste to my appointment. Well, my mind is tuned for such a scene. I shall wish only to become a principal in it, and reverse the tale my cursed folly put me upon forging here. O love!

87 *forbid* i.e., forbidden (a possible eighteenth-century usage)
91 *probation* testing

121-5 *O love . . . to madness* perhaps alludes to *A Midsummer Night's Dream*, V. i, 4-8

—tormentor!—fiend!—whose influence, like the moon's, acting on men of dull souls, makes idiots of them, but meeting subtler spirits, betrays their course, and urges sensibility to madness! *Exit*

*Enter* MAID *and* LYDIA

MAID

My mistress, Ma'am, I know, was here just now—perhaps she is only in the next room. *Exit* MAID

LYDIA

Heigh ho!—though he has used me so, this fellow runs strangely in my head. I believe one lecture from my grave cousin will make me recall him.

*Enter* JULIA

LYDIA

O Julia, I am come to you with such an appetite for consolation. Lud! child, what's the matter with you? You have been crying! I'll be hanged, if that Faulkland has not been tormenting you!

JULIA

You mistake the cause of my uneasiness—something *has* flurried me a little—nothing that you can guess at.—(*Aside*) I would not accuse Faulkland to a sister!

LYDIA

Ah! whatever vexations you may have, I can assure you mine surpass them. You know who Beverley proves to be?

JULIA

I will now own to you, Lydia, that Mr Faulkland had before informed me of the whole affair. Had young Absolute been the person you took him for, I should not have accepted your confidence on the subject, without a serious endeavour to counteract your caprice.

LYDIA

So, then, I see I have been deceived by everyone!—but I don't care—I'll never have him.

JULIA

Nay, Lydia——

LYDIA

Why, is it not provoking; when I thought we were coming to the prettiest distress imaginable, to find myself made a mere Smithfield bargain of at last.—There had I projected

---

150 *Smithfield bargain* Smithfield is the central meat market in London; a 'Smithfield bargain' is one in which the purchaser is fooled, and hence a marriage in which money rather than love is the main consideration

one of the most sentimental elopements!—so becoming a disguise!—so amiable a ladder of ropes!—conscious moon—four horses—Scotch parson—with such surprise to Mrs Malaprop—and such paragraphs in the newspapers!—Oh, I shall die with disappointment.

JULIA

I don't wonder at it!

LYDIA

Now—sad reverse!—what have I to expect, but, after a deal of flimsy preparation with a bishop's licence, and my aunt's blessing, to go simpering up to the altar; or perhaps be cried three times in a country church, and have an unmannerly fat clerk ask the consent of every butcher in the parish to join John Absolute and Lydia Languish, *spinster*! Oh, that I should live to hear myself called spinster!

JULIA

Melancholy, indeed!

LYDIA

How mortifying, to remember the dear delicious shifts I used to be put to, to gain half a minute's conversation with this fellow! How often have I stole forth, in the coldest night in January, and found him in the garden, stuck like a dripping statue! There would he kneel to me in the snow, and sneeze and cough so pathetically! he shivering with cold, and I with apprehension! and while the freezing blast numbed our joints, how warmly would he press me to pity his flame, and glow with mutual ardour!—Ah, Julia! that was something like being in love.

152 *conscious* sharing in the feelings of human beings (a vogue usage)
168 *stole* cf. 'forbid' l. 87

---

153 *Scotch parson* Until recently, in English law, people under twenty-one were not allowed to marry without their parents' or guardian's consent. No such law applied in Scotland, and hence couples eloped there to marry

158 *bishop's licence* After Hardwicke's Marriage Act of 1753, those who wished to marry could either obtain a bishop's licence, giving permission for the service in the church of the parish in which one of the parties lived, or have their banns cried three times on successive Sundays in the church they attended or wished to be married in. This latter procedure was thought an ordeal for a fashionably delicate young lady. See Dorothy Marshall, 'Manners, Meals, and Domestic Pastimes', in A. S. Turberville, ed., *Johnson's England* (Oxford, 1933), I, 353

174 *pity his flame . . . mutual ardour* poetic language

JULIA

If I were in spirits, Lydia, I should chide you only by laughing heartily at you: but it suits more the situation of my mind, at present, earnestly to entreat you, not to let a man, who loves you with sincerity, suffer that unhappiness from your caprice, which I know too well caprice can inflict.

LYDIA

O Lud! what has brought my aunt here!

*Enter* MRS MALAPROP, FAG, *and* DAVID

MRS MALAPROP

So! so! Here's fine work! Here's fine suicide, paracide, and simulation going on in the fields! and Sir Anthony not to be found to prevent the antistrophe!

JULIA

For heaven's sake, Madam, what's the meaning of this?

MRS MALAPROP

That gentleman can tell you—'twas he enveloped the affair to me.

LYDIA (*To* FAG)

Do, Sir, will you inform us.

FAG

Ma'am, I should hold myself very deficient in every requisite that forms the man of breeding, if I delayed a moment to give all the information in my power to a lady so deeply interested in the affair as you are.

LYDIA

But quick! quick, Sir!

FAG

True, Ma'am, as you say, one should be quick in divulging matters of this nature; for should we be tedious, perhaps while we are flourishing on the subject, two or three lives may be lost!

LYDIA

O patience! Do, Ma'am, for heaven's sake! tell us what is the matter?

183 *paracide* for, parricide
184 *simulation* 1776 (salivation 1775)
185 *antistrophe* one of the divisions of the Greek choral ode; for, catastrophe
187 *enveloped* wrapped up; for, developed, in the sense of revealed, unfolded (of a story)
197 *flourishing* see Prologue l. 23

MRS MALAPROP

Why, murder's the matter! slaughter's the matter! killing's the matter!—but he can tell you the perpendiculars.

LYDIA

Then, prithee, Sir, be brief.

FAG

Why then, Ma'am—as to murder—I cannot take upon me to say—and as to slaughter, or manslaughter, that will be as the jury finds it.

LYDIA

But who, Sir—who are engaged in this?

FAG

Faith, Ma'am, one is a young gentleman whom I should be very sorry anything was to happen to—a very pretty behaved gentleman! We have lived much together, and always on terms.

LYDIA

But who is this? who! who! who!

FAG

My master, Ma'am—my master—I speak of my master.

LYDIA

Heavens! What, Captain Absolute!

MRS MALAPROP

Oh, to be sure, you are frightened now!

JULIA

But who are with him, Sir?

FAG

As to the rest, Ma'am, this gentleman can inform you better than I.

JULIA (*To* DAVID)

Do speak, friend.

DAVID

Lookee, my lady—by the mass! there's mischief going on.—Folks don't use to meet for amusement with fire-arms, firelocks, fire-engines, fire-screens, fire-office, and

202 *perpendiculars* another mathematical term; for particulars

211 *on terms* an ambiguous phrase with the possible meanings of 'in a friendly way' and 'on certain conditions' (i.e., Absolute's paying Fag his wages)

222 *firelocks* muskets

222 *fire-office* fire insurance office; David is carried away by a train of association

the devil knows what other crackers besides!—This, my lady, I say, has an angry favour.

JULIA

But who is there beside Captain Absolute, friend?

DAVID

My poor master—under favour, for mentioning him first. You know me, my lady—I am David—and my master of course is, or *was*, Squire Acres. Then comes Squire Faulkland.

JULIA

Do, Ma'am, let us instantly endeavour to prevent mischief.

MRS MALAPROP

O fie—it would be very inelegant in us: we should only participate things.

DAVID

Ah! do, Mrs Aunt, save a few lives—they are desperately given, believe me. Above all, there is that bloodthirsty Philistine, Sir Lucius O'Trigger.

MRS MALAPROP

Sir Lucius O'Trigger! O mercy! have they drawn poor little dear Sir Lucius into the scrape? Why, how, how you stand, girl! you have no more feeling than one of the Derbyshire putrefactions!

LYDIA

What are we to do, Madam?

MRS MALAPROP

Why, fly with the utmost felicity to be sure, to prevent mischief: here, friend—you can show us the place?

FAG

If you please, Ma'am, I will conduct you. David, do you look for Sir Anthony. *Exit* DAVID

223 *crackers* fireworks which exploded with a sharp report

224 *favour* appearance

233 *participate* for, precipitate

236 *Philistine* like the Biblical Philistines, very belligerent (and also alien, being Irish)

242 *felicity* for, velocity

---

240 *Derbyshire putrefactions* for, petrifactions, which is used to describe both fossils in a cave at Mam Tor, and stalactites in Poole's Hole at Buxton in a contemporary guidebook (Anon., *Sketch of a Tour into Derbyshire and Yorkshire* (London, 1778), pp. 107-8 and 121)

MRS MALAPROP

Come, girls! this gentleman will exhort us. Come, Sir, you're our envoy—lead the way, and we'll precede.

FAG

Not a step before the ladies for the world!

MRS MALAPROP

You're sure you know the spot.

FAG

I think I can find it, Ma'am; and one good thing is, we shall hear the report of the pistols as we draw near, so we can't well miss them; never fear, Ma'am, never fear.

*Exeunt, he talking*

## [Act V,] Scene ii

[*Scene, the*] *South Parade*

*Enter* ABSOLUTE, *putting his sword under his greatcoat*

ABSOLUTE

A sword seen in the streets of Bath would raise as great an alarm as a mad dog. How provoking this is in Faulkland!—never punctual! I shall be obliged to go without him at last. Oh, the devil! here's Sir Anthony!—how shall I escape him?

*Muffles up his face, and takes a circle to go off*

*Enter* SIR ANTHONY

SIR ANTHONY

How one may be deceived at a little distance! Only that I see he don't know me, I could have sworn that was Jack! Hey! Gad's life, it is. Why, Jack, you dog! what are you afraid of? Hey! sure I'm right. Why, Jack—Jack Absolute!

*Goes up to him*

ABSOLUTE

Really, Sir, you have the advantage of me: I don't remember ever to have had the honour—my name is Saunderson, at your service.

246 *exhort* for, escort
247 *envoy* for, convoy (i.e., escort)
247 *precede* for, proceed
5 s.d. *takes a circle* walks round in a circle
8 *you dog* 1775 (omitted 1776)

---

1 *A sword . . . Bath* see above, III. iv, 66

SIR ANTHONY

Sir, I beg your pardon—I took you—hey!—why, zounds! it is—stay—(*Looks up to his face*) So, so—your humble servant, Mr Saunderson! Why, you scoundrel, what tricks are you after now?

ABSOLUTE

Oh! a joke, Sir, a joke! I came here on purpose to look for you, Sir.

SIR ANTHONY

You did! Well, I am glad you were so lucky: but what are you muffled up so for? What's this for?—hey?

ABSOLUTE

'Tis cool, Sir; isn't it?—rather chilly somehow: but I shall be late—I have a particular engagement.

SIR ANTHONY

Stay—why, I thought you were looking for me? Pray, Jack, where is't you are going?

ABSOLUTE

Going, Sir!

SIR ANTHONY

Aye—where are you going?

ABSOLUTE

Where am I going?

SIR ANTHONY

You unmannerly puppy!

ABSOLUTE

I was going, Sir, to—to—to—to Lydia—Sir to Lydia—to make matters up if I could; and I was looking for you, Sir, to—to——

SIR ANTHONY

To go with you, I suppose—well, come along.

ABSOLUTE

Oh! zounds! no, Sir, not for the world! I wished to meet with you, Sir, to—to—to—you find it cool, I'm sure, Sir—you'd better not stay out.

SIR ANTHONY

Cool! not at all—well, Jack—and what will you say to Lydia?

ABSOLUTE

Oh, Sir, beg her pardon, humour her—promise and vow: but I detain you, Sir—consider the cold air on your gout.

SIR ANTHONY

Oh, not at all!—not at all!—I'm in no hurry. Ah! Jack, you youngsters when once you are wounded here. (*Putting his hand to* ABSOLUTE*'s breast*) Hey! what the deuce have you got here?

ABSOLUTE

Nothing, Sir—nothing.

SIR ANTHONY

What's this?—here's something damned hard!

ABSOLUTE

Oh, trinkets, Sir! trinkets—a bauble for Lydia!

SIR ANTHONY

Nay, let me see your taste. (*Pulls his coat open, the sword falls*) Trinkets!—a bauble for Lydia! Zounds! sirrah, you are not going to cut her throat, are you?

ABSOLUTE

Ha! ha! ha!—I thought it would divert you, Sir, though I didn't mean to tell you till afterwards.

SIR ANTHONY

You didn't? Yes, this is a very diverting trinket, truly.

ABSOLUTE

Sir, I'll explain to you. You know, Sir, Lydia is romantic—devilish romantic, and very absurd of course: now, Sir, I intend, if she refuses to forgive me—to unsheath this sword—and swear—I'll fall upon its point, and expire at her feet!

SIR ANTHONY

Fall upon a fiddlestick's end! Why, I suppose it is the very thing that would please her. Get along, you fool.

ABSOLUTE

Well, Sir, you shall hear of my success—you shall hear. 'Oh, Lydia! forgive me, or this pointed steel'—says I.

SIR ANTHONY

'Oh, booby! stab away, and welcome'—says she. Get along! and damn your trinkets! *Exit* ABSOLUTE

*Enter* DAVID, *running*

DAVID

Stop him! stop him! murder! thief! fire! Stop fire! stop fire! Oh! Sir Anthony—call! call! bid 'em stop! Murder! Fire!

SIR ANTHONY

Fire! murder! where?

DAVID

Oons! he's out of sight! and I'm out of breath, for my part! Oh, Sir Anthony, why didn't you stop him? why didn't you stop him?

SIR ANTHONY

Zounds! the fellow's mad!—Stop whom? Stop Jack?

DAVID

Aye, the Captain, Sir!—there's murder and slaughter——

SIR ANTHONY

Murder!

DAVID

Aye, please you, Sir Anthony, there's all kinds of murder, all sorts of slaughter to be seen in the fields: there's fighting going on, Sir—bloody sword-and-gun fighting!

SIR ANTHONY

Who are going to fight, dunce?

DAVID

Everybody that I know of, Sir Anthony: everybody is going to fight, my poor master, Sir Lucius O'Trigger, your son, the Captain——

SIR ANTHONY

Oh, the dog! I see his tricks—do you know the place?

DAVID

Kingsmead Fields.

SIR ANTHONY

You know the way?

DAVID

Not an inch; but I'll call the mayor—aldermen—constables—churchwardens—and beadles—we can't be too many to part them.

SIR ANTHONY

Come along—give me your shoulder! We'll get assistance as we go—the lying villain! Well, I shall be in such a frenzy—so—this was the history of his damned trinkets! I'll bauble him! *Exeunt*

---

84-5 *mayor . . . beadles* David mentions all the civic officers he can think of, from the dignitaries to the lowest. Constables and beadles, before the formation of a police force, were appointed by the parish to keep the peace, but were often inefficient. In *Humphrey Clinker* a duel is prevented by the mayor and constables (ed. cit., p. 41)

87 *your shoulder* Sir Anthony requires support because of his gout

## [Act V,] Scene iii

*[Scene,] Kingsmead Fields*

SIR LUCIUS *and* ACRES, *with pistols*

ACRES

By my valour! then, Sir Lucius, forty yards is a good distance—odds levels and aims! I say it is a good distance.

SIR LUCIUS

Is it for muskets or small field-pieces? Upon my conscience, Mr Acres, you must leave those things to me. Stay now—I'll show you. (*Measures paces along the stage*) There now, that is a very pretty distance—a pretty gentleman's distance.

ACRES

Zounds! we might as well fight in a sentry-box! I tell you, Sir Lucius, the farther he is off, the cooler I shall take my aim.

SIR LUCIUS

Faith! then I suppose you would aim at him best of all if he was out of sight!

ACRES

No, Sir Lucius—but I should think forty or eight and thirty yards——

SIR LUCIUS

Pho! pho! nonsense! Three or four feet between the mouths of your pistols is as good as a mile.

ACRES

Odds bullets, no!—by my valour! there is no merit in killing him so near: do, my dear Sir Lucius, let me bring him down at a long shot: a long shot, Sir Lucius, if you love me!

SIR LUCIUS

Well—the gentleman's friend and I must settle that. But tell me now, Mr Acres, in case of an accident, is there any little will or commission I could execute for you?

ACRES

I am much obliged to you, Sir Lucius—but I don't understand——

SIR LUCIUS

Why, you may think there's no being shot at without a little risk—and if an unlucky bullet should carry a quietus

3 *field-pieces* small cannon
27 *quietus* fatal wound

with it—I say it will be no time then to be bothering you about family matters.

ACRES
A *quietus*!

SIR LUCIUS
For instance now—if that should be the case—would you choose to be pickled and sent home? or would it be the same to you to lie here in the Abbey? I'm told there is very snug lying in the Abbey.

ACRES
Pickled! Snug lying in the Abbey! Odds tremors! Sir Lucius, don't talk so!

SIR LUCIUS
I suppose, Mr Acres, you never were engaged in an affair of this kind before?

ACRES
No, Sir Lucius, never before.

SIR LUCIUS
Ah! that's a pity!—there's nothing like being used to a thing. Pray now, how would you receive the gentleman's shot?

ACRES
Odds files! I've practised that—there, Sir Lucius—there (*Puts himself in an attitude*)—a side-front, hey? Odd! I'll make myself small enough—I'll stand edge-ways.

SIR LUCIUS
Now—you're quite out—for if you stand so when I take my aim—— *Levelling at him*

ACRES
Zounds! Sir Lucius—are you sure it is not cocked?

SIR LUCIUS
Never fear.

ACRES
But—but—you don't know—it may go off of its own head!

SIR LUCIUS
Pho! be easy. Well, now if I hit you in the body, my bullet has a double chance—for if it misses a vital part on your

32 *pickled* preserved in brine (formaldehyde had not then been discovered)
43 *files* either light swords, or lines of soldiers
48 *cocked* ready to fire
50 *of its own head* spontaneously

---

33 *Abbey* Bath Abbey, begun in 1499, which contains many late eighteenth-century burial monuments including that of Beau Nash

right side—'twill be very hard if it don't succeed on the left!

ACRES

A vital part! Oh, my poor vitals!

SIR LUCIUS

But, there—fix yourself so—(*Placing him*) let him see the broad side of your full front—there—now a ball or two may pass clean through your body, and never do any harm at all.

ACRES

Clean through me!—a ball or two clean through me!

SIR LUCIUS

Aye—may they—and it is much the genteelest attitude into the bargain.

ACRES

Lookee! Sir Lucius—I'd just as lief be shot in an awkward posture as a genteel one—so, by my valour! I will stand edge-ways.

SIR LUCIUS (*Looking at his watch*)

Sure they don't mean to disappoint us. Hah? No, faith—I think I see them coming.

ACRES

Hey!—what!—coming!——

SIR LUCIUS

Aye—who are those yonder getting over the stile?

ACRES

There are two of them, indeed! Well—let them come —hey, Sir Lucius!—we—we—we—we—won't run——

SIR LUCIUS

Run!

ACRES

No—I say—we *won't* run, by my valour!

SIR LUCIUS

What the devil's the matter with you?

ACRES

Nothing—nothing—my dear friend—my dear Sir Lucius —but—I—I—I don't feel quite so bold, somehow—as I did.

SIR LUCIUS

O fie!—consider your honour.

55 *Oh, my poor vitals* 1775 (omitted 1776)
63 *lief* willingly

ACRES

Aye—true—my honour—do, Sir Lucius, hedge in a word or two every now and then about my honour.

SIR LUCIUS (*Looking*)

Well, here they're coming.

ACRES

Sir Lucius—if I wa'n't with you, I should almost think I was afraid—if my valour should leave me!—Valour will come and go.

SIR LUCIUS

Then pray keep it fast, while you have it.

ACRES

Sir Lucius—I doubt it is going—yes—my valour is certainly going!—it is sneaking off!—I feel it oozing out as it were at the palms of my hands!

SIR LUCIUS

Your honour—your honour—here they are.

ACRES

O mercy!—now—that I were safe at Clod Hall! or could be shot before I was aware!

*Enter* FAULKLAND *and* ABSOLUTE

SIR LUCIUS

Gentlemen, your most obedient—hah!—what Captain Absolute! So, I suppose, Sir, you are come here, just like myself—to do a kind office, first for your friend—then to proceed to business on your own account.

ACRES

What, Jack!—my dear Jack!—my dear friend!

ABSOLUTE

Harkee, Bob, Beverley's at hand.

SIR LUCIUS

Well, Mr Acres—I don't blame your saluting the gentleman civilly. So, Mr Beverley, (*To* FAULKLAND) if you'll choose your weapons, the Captain and I will measure the ground.

FAULKLAND

*My* weapons, Sir.

ACRES

Odds life! Sir Lucius, I'm not going to fight Mr Faulkland; these are my particular friends.

SIR LUCIUS

What, Sir, did not you come here to fight Mr Acres?

79 *hedge* 1775 (edge 1776); in the obsolete sense of 'insinuate'

FAULKLAND

Not I, upon my word, Sir.

SIR LUCIUS

Well, now, that's mighty provoking! But I hope, Mr Faulkland, as there are three of us come on purpose for the game, you won't be so cantankerous as to spoil the party by sitting out.

ABSOLUTE

O pray, Faulkland, fight to oblige Sir Lucius.

FAULKLAND

Nay, if Mr Acres is so bent on the matter.

ACRES

No, no, Mr Faulkland—I'll bear my disappointment like a Christian. Lookee, Sir Lucius, there's no occasion at all for me to fight; and if it is the same to you, I'd as lief let it alone.

SIR LUCIUS

Observe me, Mr Acres—I must not be trifled with. You have certainly challenged somebody—and you came here to fight him. Now, if that gentleman is willing to represent him—I can't see, for my soul, why it isn't just the same thing.

ACRES

Why no—Sir Lucius—I tell you, 'tis one Beverley I've challenged—a fellow, you see, that dare not show his face! if *he* were here, I'd make him give up his pretensions directly!

ABSOLUTE

Hold, Bob—let me set you right—there is no such man as Beverley in the case. The person who assumed that name is before you; and as his pretensions are the same in both characters, he is ready to support them in whatever way you please.

SIR LUCIUS

Well, this is lucky—now you have an opportunity——

ACRES

What, quarrel with my dear friend Jack Absolute—not if he were fifty Beverleys! Zounds! Sir Lucius, you would not have me be so unnatural.

SIR LUCIUS

Upon my conscience, Mr Acres, your valour has oozed away with a vengeance!

ACRES

Not in the least! Odds backs and abettors! I'll be your

137 *backs* supporters, seconds in a duel

second with all my heart—and if you should get a quietus, you may command me entirely. I'll get you a snug lying in the Abbey here; or pickle you, and send you over to Blunderbuss Hall, or anything of the kind with the greatest pleasure.

SIR LUCIUS

Pho! pho! you are little better than a coward.

ACRES

Mind, gentlemen, he calls me a coward; coward was the word, by my valour!

SIR LUCIUS

Well, Sir?

ACRES

Lookee, Sir Lucius, 'tisn't that I mind the word coward —coward may be said in joke. But if you had called me a poltroon, odds daggers and balls!

SIR LUCIUS

Well, Sir?

ACRES

—I should have thought you a very ill-bred man.

SIR LUCIUS

Pho! you are beneath my notice.

ABSOLUTE

Nay, Sir Lucius, you can't have a better second than my friend, Acres. He is a most determined dog—called in the country, 'Fighting Bob'. He generally kills a man a week; don't you, Bob?

ACRES

Aye—at home!

SIR LUCIUS

Well then, Captain, 'tis we must begin—so come out, my little counsellor, (*Draws his sword*) and ask the gentleman, whether he will resign the lady, without forcing you to proceed against him?

ABSOLUTE

Come on then, Sir; (*Draws*) since you won't let it be an amicable suit, here's my reply.

*Enter* SIR ANTHONY, DAVID, [MRS MALAPROP, LYDIA, *and* JULIA]

149 *poltroon* cowardly scoundrel
163 s.d. MRS MALAPROP, LYDIA, and JULIA ed. (and the women 1775)

163 *amicable suit* Absolute takes up Sir Lucius's legal metaphor in 'counsellor': an 'amicable suit' is one settled out of court, i.e., without a contest (here, the duel)

DAVID

Knock 'em down, sweet Sir Anthony, knock down my master in particular—and bind his hands over to their good behaviour!

SIR ANTHONY

Put up, Jack, put up, or I shall be in a frenzy—how came you in a duel, Sir?

ABSOLUTE

Faith, Sir, that gentleman can tell you better than I; 'twas he called on me, and you know, Sir, I serve his Majesty.

SIR ANTHONY

Here's a pretty fellow; I catch him going to cut a man's throat, and he tells me, he serves his Majesty!—Zounds! sirrah, then how durst you draw the King's sword against one of his subjects?

ABSOLUTE

Sir, I tell you! That gentleman called me out, without explaining his reasons.

SIR ANTHONY

Gad! Sir, how came you to call my son out, without explaining your reasons?

SIR LUCIUS

Your son, Sir, insulted me in a manner which my honour could not brook.

SIR ANTHONY

Zounds! Jack, how durst you insult the gentleman in a manner which his honour could not brook?

MRS MALAPROP

Come, come, let's have no honour before ladies. Captain Absolute, come here—how could you intimidate us so? Here's Lydia has been terrified to death for you.

ABSOLUTE

For fear I should be killed, or escape, Ma'am?

183 *honour* in the sense of 'chastity', a frequent usage in Restoration comedies in *doubles entendres* (hence Mrs Malaprop's objection)

---

165-6 *bind his hands . . . behaviour* David comically interjects the important parts (the hands) into the common phrase, to bind someone over to his good behaviour, i.e., to require a promise of good behaviour

170 *I serve his Majesty* The *Articles of War* in fact prohibited officers from engaging in duels, acting as seconds, carrying challenges, and from upbraiding others for refusing to duel. These prohibitions were totally disregarded, since the unwritten code of honour would condemn as a coward an officer who refused a challenge (some men who did refuse to duel were even tried by court martial for 'conduct unbecoming', despite the *Articles*)

MRS MALAPROP

Nay, no delusions to the past—Lydia is convinced; speak child.

SIR LUCIUS

With your leave, Ma'am, I must put in a word here—I believe I could interpret the young lady's silence. Now mark——

LYDIA

What is it you mean, Sir?

SIR LUCIUS

Come, come, Delia, we must be serious now—this is no time for trifling.

LYDIA

'Tis true, Sir; and your reproof bids me offer this gentleman my hand, and solicit the return of his affections.

ABSOLUTE

Oh! my little angel, say you so?—Sir Lucius, I perceive there must be some mistake here—with regard to the affront which you affirm I have given you—I can only say, that it could not have been intentional. And as you must be convinced, that I should not fear to support a real injury—you shall now see that I am not ashamed to atone for an inadvertency—I ask your pardon. But for this lady, while honoured with her approbation, I will support my claim against any man whatever.

SIR ANTHONY

Well said, Jack, and I'll stand by you, my boy.

ACRES

Mind, I give up all my claim—I make no pretensions to anything in the world—and if I can't get a wife, without fighting for her, by my valour! I'll live a bachelor.

SIR LUCIUS

Captain, give me your hand—an affront handsomely acknowledged becomes an obligation—and as for the lady—if she chooses to deny her own handwriting here——*Taking out letters*

MRS MALAPROP

Oh, he will dissolve my mystery! Sir Lucius, perhaps there's some mistake—perhaps, I can illuminate——

SIR LUCIUS

Pray, old gentlewoman, don't interfere, where you have

187 *delusions* for, allusions
213 s.d. *Taking out letters* 1775 (Takes out letters 1776)
214 *dissolve* in the archaic sense of 'resolve'

no business. Miss Languish, are you my Delia, or not?

LYDIA

Indeed, Sir Lucius, I am not.

LYDIA *and* ABSOLUTE *walk aside*

MRS MALAPROP

Sir Lucius O'Trigger—ungrateful as you are—I own the soft impeachment—pardon my blushes, I am Delia.

SIR LUCIUS

You Delia—pho! pho! be easy.

MRS MALAPROP

Why, thou barbarous Vandyke—those letters are mine. When you are more sensible of my benignity—perhaps I may be brought to encourage your addresses.

SIR LUCIUS

Mrs Malaprop, I am extremely sensible of your condescension; and whether you or Lucy have put this trick upon me, I am equally beholden to you. And to show you I'm not ungrateful, Captain Absolute! since you have taken that lady from me, I'll give you my Delia into the bargain.

ABSOLUTE

I am much obliged to you, Sir Lucius; but here's our friend, Fighting Bob, unprovided for.

SIR LUCIUS

Hah! little Valour—here, will you make your fortune?

ACRES

Odds wrinkles! No. But give me your hand, Sir Lucius, forget and forgive; but if ever I give you a chance of pickling me again, say Bob Acres is a dunce, that's all.

SIR ANTHONY

Come, Mrs Malaprop, don't be cast down—you are in your bloom yet.

MRS MALAPROP

O Sir Anthony!—men are all barbarians——

*All retire but* JULIA *and* FAULKLAND

JULIA

He seems dejected and unhappy—not sullen—there was some foundation, however, for the tale he told me—O woman! how true should be your judgment, when your resolution is so weak!

220 *impeachment* accusation (especially of treason)

221 *be easy* don't be so eager

222 *Vandyke* from the name of the painter, applied to features characteristic of his portraits; for, vandal

FAULKLAND

Julia!—how can I sue for what I so little deserve? I dare not presume—yet hope is the child of penitence.

JULIA

Oh! Faulkland, you have not been more faulty in your unkind treatment of me, than I am now in wanting inclination to resent it. As my heart honestly bids me place my weakness to the account of love, I should be ungenerous not to admit the same plea for yours.

FAULKLAND

Now I shall be blest indeed!

SIR ANTHONY *comes forward*

SIR ANTHONY

What's going on here? So you have been quarrelling too, I warrant. Come, Julia, I never interfered before; but let me have a hand in the matter at last. All the faults I have ever seen in my friend Faulkland, seemed to proceed from what he calls the *delicacy* and *warmth* of his affection for you—there, marry him directly, Julia, you'll find he'll mend surprisingly!

*The rest come forward*

SIR LUCIUS

Come now, I hope there is no dissatisfied person, but what is content; for as I have been disappointed myself, it will be very hard if I have not the satisfaction of seeing other people succeed better——

ACRES

You are right, Sir Lucius. So, Jack, I wish you joy—Mr Faulkland the same. Ladies, come now, to show you I'm neither vexed nor angry, odds tabors and pipes! I'll order the fiddles in half an hour, to the New Rooms—and I insist on your all meeting me there.

SIR ANTHONY

Gad! Sir, I like your spirit; and at night we single lads will drink a health to the young couples, and a husband to Mrs Malaprop.

FAULKLAND

Our partners are stolen from us, Jack—I hope to be congratulated by each other—yours for having checked in

---

270 *Our partners are stolen from us* i.e., Lydia and Julia are talking together, at a distance from Jack and Faulkland

time the errors of an ill-directed imagination, which might have betrayed an innocent heart; and mine, for having, by her gentleness and candour, reformed the unhappy temper of one, who by it made wretched whom he loved most, and tortured the heart he ought to have adored.

ABSOLUTE

Well, Faulkland, we have both tasted the bitters, as well as the sweets, of love—with this difference only, that *you* always prepared the bitter cup for yourself, while I——

LYDIA

Was always obliged to me for it, hey! Mr Modesty?—But come, no more of that—our happiness is now as unallayed as general.

JULIA

Then let us study to preserve it so: and while hope pictures to us a flattering scene of future bliss, let us deny its pencil those colours which are too bright to be lasting. When hearts deserving happiness would unite their fortunes, virtue would crown them with an unfading garland of modest, hurtless flowers; but ill-judging passion will force the gaudier rose into the wreath, whose thorn offends them, when its leaves are dropped!

*Finis*

## EPILOGUE

BY THE AUTHOR

*Spoken by Mrs Bulkley*

Ladies for you—I heard our poet say—
He'd try to coax some moral from his play:
'One moral's plain'—cried I—'without more fuss;
Man's social happiness all rests on us—
Through all the drama—whether damned or not—
Love gilds the scene, and women guide the plot.
From every rank obedience is our due—
D'ye doubt?—the world's great stage shall prove it true'.
The cit—well skilled to shun domestic strife—
Will sup abroad; but first—he'll ask his wife:
John Trot, his friend, for once, will do the same,
But then—he'll just 'step home to tell my dame'.
The surly squire at noon resolves to rule,
And half the day—'Zounds! Madam is a fool!'
Convinced at night—the vanquished victor says,
'Ah! Kate! you women have such coaxing ways!'
The jolly toper chides each tardy blade,
Till reeling Bacchus calls on love for aid:
Then with each toast, he sees fair bumpers swim,
And kisses Chloe on the sparkling brim!
Nay, I have heard that statesmen—great and wise—
Will sometimes counsel with a lady's eyes;
The servile suitors watch her various face,

9 *cit* more or less contemptuous term for a denizen of the city (of London), hence, a tradesman

10 *abroad* not at home

11 *John Trot* stupid, boorish man; cf. Sir Fopling Flutter's footman in Etherege's *The Man of Mode* (1676), III. iii

12 *my dame* 1775 (his dame 1776)

17 *toper* hard drinker

17 *blade* free and easy fellow; a drinking companion

---

15 *vanquished victor* Dryden, 'Alexander's Feast', 114-15

17-20 *The jolly toper . . . sparkling brim* The hard drinker scolds his companions for drinking too slowly, until they have drunk so much that they need some stimulus to continue, i.e., the drinking of toasts to ladies, so that each time a sweetheart is toasted (Chloe is a generic name), another glass is drained, and the toper 'kisses Chloe' in the senses that he touches the glass, as it were inscribed with her name, and is grateful to her for stimulating drinking

She smiles preferment—or she frowns disgrace,
Curtsies a pension here—there nods a place.
Nor with less awe, in scenes of humbler life,
Is viewed the mistress, or is heard the wife.
The poorest peasant of the poorest soil,
The child of poverty, and heir to toil—
Early from radiant love's impartial light,
Steals one small spark, to cheer his world of night:
Dear spark! that oft through winter's chilling woes,
Is all the warmth his little cottage knows!
The wand'ring tar—who, not for years, has pressed
The widowed partner of his day of rest—
On the cold deck—far from her arms removed—
Still hums the ditty which his Susan loved:
And while around the cadence rude is blown,
The boatswain whistles in a softer tone.
The soldier, fairly proud of wounds and toil,
Pants for the triumph of his Nancy's smile;
But ere the battle should he list her cries,
The lover trembles—and the hero dies!
That heart, by war and honour steeled to fear,
Droops on a sigh, and sickens at a tear!
But ye more cautious—ye nice judging few,
Who give to beauty only beauty's due,
Though friends to love—ye view with deep regret
Our conquests marred—our triumphs incomplete,
Till polished wit more lasting charms disclose,
And judgment fix the darts which beauty throws!
—In female breasts did sense and merit rule,
The lover's mind would ask no other school;
Shamed into sense—the scholars of our eyes,
Our beaux from *gallantry* would soon be wise;
Would gladly light, their homage to improve,
The lamp of knowledge at the torch of love!

40 *fairly* justly
55 *gallantry* devotion to ladies

# APPENDIX

*Lydia's Books*

I.ii, 4 *The Reward of Constancy* possibly, *Female Constancy; or, the History of Miss Arabella Waldegrave* (1769), or *The Happy Pair, or Virtue and Constancy Rewarded* (1771)

I.ii, 6 *The Fatal Connection* by Mrs Fogerty, 1773

I.ii, 8 *The Mistakes of the Heart* by Pierre Henri Treyssac de Vergy, 1769

I.ii, 11 *The Delicate Distress* by Elizabeth Griffith, 1769

I.ii, 22 *The Gordian Knot* by Richard Griffith, 1769

I.ii, 23 *Peregrine Pickle* by Tobias Smollett, 1751

I.ii, 23 *The Tears of Sensibility* translated from the French by J. Murdoch, 1773

I.ii, 24 *Humphrey Clinker* by Tobias Smollett, 1771

I.ii, 24 *The Memoirs of a Lady of Quality* included in *Peregrine Pickle,* or *Memoirs of an unfortunate Lady of Quality*, 1774

I.ii, 26 *The Sentimental Journey* by Laurence Sterne, 1768

I.ii, 28 *The Whole Duty of Man* a lengthy religious handbook, probably by Richard Allestree, first published in 1659, which went into many editions in the eighteenth century

I.ii, 160 *Roderick Random* by Tobias Smollett, 1748

I.ii, 161 *The Innocent Adultery* possibly, *Harriet;* or, *the Innocent Adulteress,* 1771

I.ii, 162 *Lord Aimworth The History of Lord Aimsworth and the Hon. Charles Hartford*, 1773

I.ii, 163 *Ovid* perhaps *Ovid's Art of Love*, a collection of translations, first published in 1709, which was very popular in the eighteenth century

I.ii, 164 *The Man of Feeling* by Henry Mackenzie, 1771

I.ii, 165 *Mrs Chapone* a blue-stocking, whose *Letters on the Improvement of the Mind* were published in 1773

I.ii, 165 *Fordyce's Sermons* James Fordyce, *Sermons to Young Women*, 1765. He disapproves of novels. See E. E. Phare, 'Lydia Languish, Lydia Bennet, and Dr Fordyce's Sermons', *Notes and Queries* CCIX (1964), 183

I.ii, 169 *Lord Chesterfield's Letters* written by the fourth Earl of Chesterfield to his illegitimate son, published 1774: an odd choice for 'respectable' reading, since Dr Johnson condemned them as teaching 'the morals of a whore, and the manners of a dancing master'. (Boswell's *Life*, ed. cit., I, 266)

*Songs*

II.i, 209 *When absent from my soul's delight* from *Twelve Songs Set to Music by William Jackson of Exeter Opera Quarta* (London, n.d.), Song VI:

When absent from my Soul's Delight,
What Terrors fill my troubled Breast,
What Terrors fill my troubled Breast:
Once more return'd to thy love's Sight,
Hope too returns, my Fears have rest,
Hope too returns, my Fears have rest.

II.i, 211 *Go, gentle gales* from the same volume, Song V:

Go gentle Gales go gentle Gales and bear my sighs away,
To Delia's Ear to Delia's Ear the tender Notes convey.
As some sad Turtle his lost love deplores,
And with deep Murmurs fills the sounding Shores,
Thus far from Delia to the Woods I mourn to the Woods I mourn.
Alike unheard, unpitied, alike unheard, unpitied, and forlorn.
(from Pope's 'Autumn, The Third Pastoral' 17-22)

II.i, 213 *My heart's my own* from Isaac Bickerstaff, *Love in a Village: A Comic Opera* (1762), I. i, Air III:

My heart's my own, my will is free,
  And so shall be my voice;
No mortal man shall wed with me,
  'Till first he's made my choice.
Let parents rule cry nature's laws,
  And children still obey;
And is there then no saving clause,
  Against tyrannic sway.

IV.iv, 157 *Youth's the season* from John Gay, *The Beggar's Opera* (1728), II. iv, Air XXII (sung by Macheath and a chorus of whores):

Youth's the Season made for Joys,
  Love is then our Duty,
She alone who that employs,
  Well deserves her Beauty.
Let's be gay,
  While we may,
Beauty's a Flower, despis'd in decay.

(Chorus) Youth's the Season, &c.
Let us drink and sport to-day,
Ours is not tomorrow.
Love with Youth flies swift, away,
Age is nought but Sorrow.
Dance and sing,
Time's on the Wing,
Life never knows the return of Spring.
(Chorus) Let us drink, &c.

*Printed by The Garden City Press Limited*
*Letchworth, Hertfordshire SG6 1JS*